Society and the Curriculum
in Australia

Classroom and Curriculum in Australia

A series edited by Malcolm Skilbeck which sets out to remedy the lack of Australian material in an important and fast-growing area—*Curriculum*. The intention is to put the theory and the research on numerous aspects of Curriculum firmly into the *classroom* setting, and to provide teachers with material which will help them understand a complex field.

The series will include books on:

Individual Differences (published)
Teachers as Curriculum Evaluators
Society and Curriculum in Australia
Curriculum Development and the School
Basic Curriculum

Other books by P.W. Musgrave:

Sociology of Education
Technical Education, Education, and the Labour Force
Society and Education in English since 1800
The School as an Organisation
The Economic Structure
Society, History and Education: A Reader (editor)
Knowledge, the Curriculum and Change
Contemporary Studies in the Curriculum (editor)
Alternative Schools (edited with R.J.W. Selleck)
Participation in Schools? (with R.T. Fitzgerald and D.W. Pettit)
The Moral Curriculum

Classroom and Curriculum in Australia: No 2

Series Editor: Malcolm Skilbeck, Director,
Curriculum Development Centre

Society and the Curriculum in Australia

P.W. MUSGRAVE
Professor of Education, Monash University

SYDNEY
GEORGE ALLEN & UNWIN
LONDON   BOSTON

First published in 1979 by
George Allen & Unwin Australia Pty Ltd
8 Napier Street
North Sydney NSW 2060

National Library of Australia
Cataloguing-in-Publication entry:

Musgrave, Peter William.
  Society & the curriculum in Australia.

  (Classroom and curriculum in Australia; 2)
  Index
  Bibliography
  ISBN 0 86861 025 9
  ISBN 0 86861 033 x Paperback

  1. Education—Australia—Curricula. I. Title. (Series).

301.56'0994

Library of Congress Catalog Card Number: 78-71105

Set in 10 on 11.5 point Times and printed in Australia by
Printed in Hong Kong by Everbest Printing Co., Ltd.

Contents

List of Tables

Introduction

I was asked to write this book by Dr Malcolm Skilbeck of the Curriculum Development Centre, Canberra. He wanted me to write it 'from the shoulder' without the usual scholarly apparatus of footnotes. I have felt the need to indicate some of my sources in bibliographies at the end of each chapter for two reasons: to express my gratitude to the authors concerned and to guide readers concerning where they might seek further material on the topics involved.

During writing this book I read Durkheim's *The Evolution of Educational Thought'* (London: Routledge & Kegan Paul, 1977). Durkheim set himself the ambitious task of analysing curricular development in France from the Roman Empire until about 1900; I hope that this little book can be seen as the first sketch for a similar analysis of the Australian curricular experience since the first European settlement. In acknowledgement of this I have headed each chapter with a quotation from Durkheim's fascinating book.

I wish to thank the following who played some part in helping me to complete this book: my colleague, Professor Dick Selleck, who, as always, has been generous in helping with sources and who commented on the first outline of this work; Emeritus Professor Bill Connell, who read and made helpful comments on the first full draft; Dr Malcolm Skilbeck, who acted as a tactful and most helpful editor; a number of students who have studied for higher degrees with me in the area of the curriculum and who gave me ideas and materials—the only footnotes used here refer to them; and Mrs Val Newson, Mrs Elspeth Sinclair, Mrs Connie Stuart and my wife who, in the midst of their other work, have typed the various drafts of this book.

Monash University
June 1978   P.W.M.

7

1. Introduction to the Practical Problem

We cannot understand present-day humanity except in relation to that which has preceded it.

(E. Durkheim, 1977: 333)

The aim of this book is to uncover the social forces that have been and are at work on the curriculum of schools in Australia. There are a number of dimensions to this problem and the easiest way to raise the important issues involved is to give brief descriptions of some curricula from Australian schools, both past and present. After citing four such examples the nature of the practical problem that must be examined can be made clear.

1. Some Examples of Curricula of Australian Schools

In their Fourth Report (1856–57) the Commissioners for National Education for the Colony of Victoria included some recommendations for curricula in elementary schools drawn from a circular, dated 1853. Table 1.1, showing recommended times in hours and minutes per day for specific subjects, is based upon this material; it indicates in outline the content of the curriculum suggested and the priority given to the individual parts.

The first quarter of an hour of each school day was to be spent in 'Preparation for Business; Inspection as to Personal Cleanliness'. The most cursory examination of the 22 hours 55 minutes of weekly teaching involved in this timetable raises a number of questions. For example, why were the recommendations for girls so different from those for boys? Or why were Geography and Singing included, but certain other subjects, which today would be seen to have an equal claim, omitted, e.g. History and Physical Education?

In 1925 the regulations of the New South Wales Education

TABLE 1.1 *Time Allocations—Victorian Elementary School, 1850s*

(hours and minutes per day)

	The Boys School		The Girls School	
	Forms I–III	Forms IV–V	Form I	Forms II–IV
English	2.20	1.50	2.00	1.15
Arithmetic	1.00	1.30	0.30	0.45
Geography	0.30	0.30	—	0.30
Geography or English	—	—	—	0.30
Singing	0.30	0.30	0.30	0.30
Sewing	—	—	1.20	1.20
Time in School	4.20	4.20	4.20	4.20

Source: A.G. Austin and R.J.W. Selleck (1975), p. 33

Department suggested the time allocations shown in Table 1.2 for each year in elementary schools. These suggestions relate to the time to be given to specified teaching subjects and ignore about ten hours per week allowed for proceedings such as assemblies and for free time.

TABLE 1.2 *Time Allocations—N.S.W. Elementary Schools, 1925*

(hours and minutes per week)

Grades	1	2	3	4	5	6
English	10.00	10.00	8.00	8.00	7.00	7.00
Mathematics	3.00	3.00	4.00	4.00	4.00	4.00
Nature Knowledge	2.00	2.00	2.30	2.30	2.45	3.00
Morals & Civics	1.30	1.30	2.15	2.15	3.00	3.00
Art & Manual Work	3.45	3.45	3.30	3.30	3.30	3.30
Music	1.30	1.30	1.30	1.30	1.30	1.15
Physical Training	2.00	2.00	2.00	2.00	2.00	2.00
Totals	23.45	23.45	23.45	23.45	23.45	23.45

Source: P.R. Cole, ed. (1932), p. 197

Not only are the recommended allocations of time to various subjects different from those for Victorian elementary schools of the 1850s, but also new subjects, including Nature Knowledge, Art and Physical Training, have been introduced into these schools. Furthermore no longer, it seems, are girls differentiated from boys.

Table 1.2, required subjects and suggested time allocations, can be compared with the recommendations then current in some other Australian States and, perhaps not quite so accurately, with the situation in the United States of America, as shown in Table 1.3.

TABLE 1.3 *Some Comparisons of Time Allocations, 1920s*

(% of total hours)

Occupation	N.S.W.	Victoria	South Australia	U.S.A.
Three R's	50.5	66.0	70.2	49.2
Content Subjects	19.8	12.8	11.5	13.4
Special Subjects	29.6	21.2	18.2	37.4
Totals	99.9	100.0	99.9	100.0

Source: P.R. Cole, ed. (1932), p. 198

Table 1.3 makes clear the remarkable differences between States within Australia and between the situation existing in Australia and that claimed to be ruling in the United States of America. But a new set of questions is also raised. For example, does the apparently different focus on the three R's in the four sets of recommendations hide different ways of teaching literacy and numeracy in each Australian State and in the United States of America? And are the so-called Content and Special Subjects the same in all States?

The two examples cited so far have related to what was formerly known as elementary education. What of the curriculum in the secondary school? For historical reasons to which some attention will be paid in Chapters 3 and 4, private schools have had great influence upon the growth and nature of Australian secondary schools. Therefore the first example at this level of education to be cited here is from an independent school. In the early 1950s Melbourne Church of England Girls Grammar School was considered rather progressive in the type of secondary schooling that it offered. In Forms I and II, with some minor exceptions, all students undertook a common course of study, but from Form III onwards each student's course contained the following elements: common periods taken in the home classroom; periods when girls worked in a set of students from various classes; periods not taken in the home classroom; and unallotted periods. The distribution between categories for Forms I to IV is shown in Table 1.4.

In Form I the common core periods covered: English (6 periods), Social Studies (6), Scripture (1), Singing (2), Physical Education and Health (5), Form Committee (1), Science (2), Library (1), Art (2), Manual Art (2), Arithmetic (5), Introduction to Mathematics (2), Introduction to Languages (3), Free Choice Periods (2). By the fifth

TABLE 1.4 *Allocation to Core and Other Purposes—*
Melbourne Girls Grammar School

(no. of periods)

Form	Common Class Periods	Sets, Others, Spares	Totals
I	35	5	40
II	25	15	40
III	21	19	40
IV	15	25	40

year the curriculum was divided so that students were placed in either academic or practical forms. The core consisted of: English (5), Singing (1), Physical Education (2), Form Committee (1), Scripture (1), to which were added for the practical forms Social Studies (5) and Biology (7). The remaining 30 periods for the academic forms consisted of choices from a large number of options (5 periods each), e.g. Mathematics, Physics, Agricultural Science, French, Latin, Greek (if needed), Greek and Roman History, Art, Social Studies and Musical Appreciation. For the practical forms the remaining eighteen periods could be chosen from a smaller range of options (5 periods each, except where specified), e.g. Domestic Science, French, Art, Craft, Typing and Shorthand (9), Bookkeeping (2), Dressmaking (2). (K.S. Cunningham and D.J. Ross, 1967: 61–71).

If one compares the details of the two curricula for elementary schools that were cited earlier with what was offered at Melbourne Girls Grammar School in the early 1950s there is clearly a growth in the range and complexity of offerings over the period of some seventy-five years, but the bare outline of the curriculum presented here does not fully portray the richness of experience possible at this girls independent school. A whole new series of questions can be raised. For example, why are options permitted? Why is such a range of subjects taught? Why is there a differentiation into academic and practical classes? In addition, at this school Scripture and Form Committee, which allowed students to participate in running the school, are included; why is this overt 'moral' dimension compulsorily included in the curriculum? Furthermore a more detailed considera- tion of the curriculum, especially for Forms V and VI, would show a relationship to certain external examinations. Why was this the case?

As a final example some details of the curriculum of a Victorian country high school in 1977 will be presented. At Form One level the curriculum was divided into three parts. All students undertook eight hours per week of General Studies with one teacher; during these periods the traditional subjects of English, History and Geography were linked together and taught as one subject. Secondly, twelve hours per week were given to a number of Specialised Subjects; these were Science, Mathematics, Comparative Languages, Music, Library and Physical Education. Finally, students spent five hours per week doing Integrated Craft, which included Art, Cookery, Needlecraft, Material Studies, Woodcraft and Graphic Communication; all students, both boys and girls, undertook six weeks, that is thirty hours, work in each subject.

A common core of a similar nature was available up to Form Three, though choice was allowed between French and Italian. In Form Four Shorthand/Typing became available and there was a special Form Five Secretarial Course, almost entirely taken by girls. Most of those in Form Six were studying towards the Higher School Certificate— the university matriculation examination—and the one common subject was English Expression, prescribed as a prerequisite for matriculation. The other four subjects could be chosen from a range of the more usual humanities and sciences together with Australian History, Art, Legal Studies, French and Italian.

Examination of this curriculum and comparison with the first example of a secondary curriculum raise a further set of questions. For example, this is a somewhat smaller school, but is the narrower range of subjects offered merely related to size? Why is the degree of choice available to students less in this high school than in the independent school? Is it true that there is no overt moral element in this school's curriculum? Why are the languages chosen for inclusion here French and Italian? Have examinations exercised a greater influence here than at Melbourne Girls Grammar School? And, finally, are boys and girls really treated in the same way now in state high schools?

One could go on citing different curricula from past and from present practice. In particular, no example has been given from the so-called progressive schools where in general much more choice is available to students, particularly at the secondary level, and where the range of offerings is very wide, often including considerable periods of experience outside the classroom in the community within which the school is set. However the four examples cited have raised sufficient important questions of detail to demonstrate the range of issues which this book will examine.

2. The Practical Problem

Our main concern is the way in which social factors influence the curriculum: individuals make decisions about what is to be taught in schools, but in doing so they are usually influenced by others or by forces beyond their control. Although there is some tendency today to forget that individuals can and do change what goes on in any society, yet social forces are immensely powerful and it is upon them that the main, but not the whole, focus of analysis will be put here.

The four examples of curricula that have been given have raised a host of detailed questions. These may be subsumed under four dimensions of the general problem:

i) What influence does the past have upon the present? There were both continuities and differences in the examples that have been given. For example, English and Mathematics in some form or other, though with differing emphasis as demonstrated by the number of periods allocated, were found throughout the time considered and at all age ranges, but Science was not. Again, Latin seems to have disappeared from recent curricula in many secondary schools; though this is not the case in the two examples given. Japanese and Indonesian are now taught in some schools. Furthermore, subtle changes in nomenclature have occurred through time; thus Physical Training has come to be called Physical Education. Do such changes indicate any important real change in meaning? And, if so, what? And why have they occurred through time?

ii) What changes are influencing the curriculum today? In terms of methodology one can seek explanations of social change either by tracing what happens through time or by looking for differences in what is now going on. When such differences have been isolated, an attempt can be made to locate the reasons for the variety discovered. Thus a comparison of the two secondary curricula, one of which was considered progressive in the mid-1950s and the other of which, though dated 1977, could have been found in the same State in the 1960s, raises some interesting questions. Why was Agricultural Science taught in a metropolitan and not a rural school? Why was Italian taught in the rural and not the metropolitan school? What place has moral and/or religious education in state and private schools?

iii) Where did the influences come from to change the curriculum or to create contemporaneous differences or to support given contemporary variations in different schools? Australia has a society rooted deeply in Europe, or, perhaps more accurately, rooted in Europe as mediated through Britain. There is, therefore, a high probability that much of what happens in schools, including the curricula, will have been deeply influenced by what has happened in Britain. But have other societies also influenced Australian curricula? Furthermore how much influence has there been from developments in Australian society itself? And what sections of Australian society have been influential? iv) Finally, what place have individuals had as opposed to social forces, in influencing the curriculum? No one can read far in nineteenth century educational history without meeting the name of Thomas Arnold, the headmaster of Rugby School from 1828–42. Again, some administrators have had great influence upon the development of educational systems. A case in point would be Sir James Kay-Shuttleworth, who between 1839 and 1849 established what was to become the British ministry responsible for education. Can similar figures, teachers or administrators or even academics, be found in Australia? And how true is it to represent such individuals as exercising what may be termed educational creativity rather than as acting as mediators for existing social forces or as interpreters of the ideas of other and more creative persons?

3. Conclusions

This chapter has indicated the immense range of problems that can be raised in trying to discuss the social forces at work on the curriculum of schools in Australia. This major problem will be tackled in this book by examining both historical change and differences at individual points in time in past as well as in present Australian curricula.

A set of general questions has been posed that covers the numerous very detailed questions that were raised as exemplars concerning the four cited curricula. These related to the influence of the past on the present, the nature of contemporary changes, the source of change and the place of individuals in curricular change. But a general problem such as that to be analysed here cannot be faced without some sort of conceptual framework—some would call it a theory, though, since prediction is usually impossible with such tools of analysis, I will not do so. In the next chapter this framework will be established. Its nature will determine what data will be brought forward for analysis. This is an important point. Much of the data will, perforce, be historical in nature, though a Victorian inevitably illustrates his argument by drawing predominantly upon examples from his own State. Yet Chapters 3, 4 and 5 must not be seen as purely historical, but more as the validation of the framework suggested. When once the framework has been seen to be sound there is the possibility of useful analysis of and practical suggestion concerning future curricular change. It is to this important matter that the final two chapters will be devoted. And it is because this is the ultimate aim of this little book that the first chapter has been entitled 'Introduction to the Practical Problem'.

Bibliography

AUSTIN A.G. and SELLECK R.J.W. (1975): *The Australian Government School 1830–1914*. Pitman: Carlton (Vic.). This book consists of a series of historical documents together with four introductions, by the editors, to successive periods of educational history. There will be several references to this work here and it forms an excellent source of historical material on the Australian curriculum.

Other References

COLE P.R. ed. (1932): *The Primary School Curriculum in Australia*. Melbourne University Press: Melbourne.
CUNNINGHAM K.S. and ROSS, D.J. (1967): *An Australian School at Work*. Australian Council for Educational Research: Hawthorn (Vic.).

2. A Perspective on Curricular Formation

> Educational transformations are always the result and the symptom of the social transformations in terms of which they are to be explained.
>
> (E. Durkheim, 1977: 166)

1. Introduction: Some Concepts

In the last chapter no definition of the curriculum was given though there was little doubt from the context about how the term was being used, namely to cover whatever knowledge those in charge of a school or of an educational system purposefully set out to pass on to their students as a result of the learning experiences that they arranged within formal settings. Another way of conceptualising this definition is to say that the curriculum consists of that selection from the whole stock of knowledge available to a society which those in power in the educational system aim to pass on to succeeding generations. This second way of defining the curriculum implicitly makes use of the concept of culture in its sociological sense. Sociologists restrict the meaning of culture to the learnt behaviour and results of such learnt behaviour available in any one society. The Australian culture, or the stock of Australian knowledge, then, consists amongst other things of knowledge about or experiences of modern science, Aboriginal artifacts, bush ballads, cricket and Australian rules, the Melbourne Cup, the Sydney Harbour Bridge, Holden cars, pavlovas and ANZAC Day.

There is no doubt that schools teach both more and less than their acknowledged curriculum. They teach less because for all sorts of reasons some students fail to learn as is expected or hoped; in this connection much attention has been given, for example, to the underachieving of members of the lower social classes. Schools teach

17

more because there are sometimes unanticipated effects of the formal structures that they create to fulfil the aims of their intended curriculum; this effect has recently been given much attention and is generally conceptualised as the hidden or latent curriculum. Although these two effects will receive some passing mention, their analysis is in both cases logically dependent upon the clear establishment of what may perhaps be called the manifest or open curriculum and it is the influence of society upon this declared curriculum that is our concern here.

At this point one other categorisation must be made, and, again, an implicit reference was made to it in Chapter 1 when considering the curriculum of the independent secondary school. The curriculum may have the aim of influencing two different dimensions of knowledge, namely those relating to academic or to moral behaviour. In the former case knowledge, the results of knowledge, and its application to abstract or logical problems is involved; in the latter case the knowledge to be learnt relates to social behaviour, that is to behaviour towards others. In practice there is often some difficulty in deciding whether a specific part of the curriculum relates to the academic or to the moral dimension. For example, knowledge about human sexuality may be taught as part of the academic curriculum, but a student may use his knowledge in his social behaviour. However for our purposes the categories will be used broadly to differentiate whether some part of the curriculum is seen as relating in the main to the individual's stock of knowledge or to how he uses this stock in interacting with others.

In the next section we shall start our analysis of the curriculum by examining the situation in which no change is occurring. At least in logic there is the possibility of seeing the curriculum to be in a state of stability. This may be the case for various reasons: for example, because no one wants to change it; or because many want to change it, but agreement seems impossible about what should be done; or, finally, because, though some disagree with what is now done, they have not the power to bring about change.

When once the existing curriculum has been challenged change is possible. The challenge, though mediated through an individual or a group, may be analysed along two dimensions. Firstly, the analysis may focus upon changes in the social structure of the society concerned, and through these structural changes the attempt may be made to trace apparent determinants, or, secondly, the focus may be upon ideological changes. These two ways of examining change will be considered in the third section of this chapter prior to a discussion of the specific dimensions of curricular change itself.

2. So-called Stability

The curriculum is under the immediate control of those in schools or of those who have power over formal educational systems. In the latter case administrators outside the schools may lay down in great detail what is to be taught in the schools. There is, however, some room for variation in this situation as head teachers may enforce the official curriculum with more or less rigour and as teachers have some power over the details to be taught and particularly over the methods to be used.

Even when such detailed control is not exercised, those involved in implementing curricular prescriptions may take for granted the existing curriculum and not wish to make any or much change in it. This consensual situation is one which formerly was assumed by some theorists, and by many of those in power outside the schools, to be normal and desirable. It is an empirical question whether in fact such a situation has ever existed though there are some reasons for believing that there may be a tendency towards such a position.

The first reason that can be given for ready acceptance of a curriculum imposed upon schools from outside is that teachers have not themselves the competence to develop their own curricula. This may well be the case in such developing societies as early nineteenth century Australia or contemporary Papua New Guinea. In addition, there may be factors working for consensual stability in the case of individual teachers. Thus a teacher may be lethargic, or too insecure or unimaginative in personality to make a curricular innovation.

Many of the characteristics of the personality of individuals that are seen by lay persons to be best analysed in psychological terms are often also explainable using the sociological concept of socialisation. This term is used to explain the way in which members of groups come to hold similar views or, at a deeper level, to have similar personalities. Members of many occupations undergo a long training, often in formal educational institutions in a great measure isolated from the world at large. Examples are the clergy, all levels of the armed forces, and teachers. Many of the assumptions about what should be taught, in both the academic and the moral curriculum, are learnt by intending teachers whilst in training and are only with great difficulty questioned thereafter, when once the busy hurly-burly of the classroom has been encountered.

Perhaps the strongest factor working for stability in the curriculum relates to the great armoury of social sanctions that operate to force the teacher to comply with what those with power over the schools wish. There are utilitarian sanctions. Thus to make many changes a teacher needs new textbooks, equipment, materials, and he may want to use different and more expensive methods of teaching, although he rarely controls enough funds to enable him to procure the requirements needed for his new curriculum.

There are, in addition, normative sanctions which depend upon the mutual acceptance by all those involved of a set of assumptions, values and beliefs. Thus the teacher may never question the authority of those over him to tell him what is to be considered worthwhile knowledge and how he is to teach it. The authority of the book and of the expert in pedagogy or curricular development is accepted utterly. In the case of moral knowledge he may accept the general behavioural standards of the age and, therefore, without question agree to the moral curriculum of the school.

However, finally, coercion may be involved in curricular stability. A teacher may not agree with the academic curriculum, but knows that, if he does not teach what is laid down or accepted as the norm, he is liable to lose his position. Many members of the community have strong views about both the academic and the moral curriculum and are willing and able to exert pressure upon those in control of the schools to ensure the continued teaching of what they see as right. Because of this a teacher who disagreed with what he might see as the rote learning of *The One Day of the Year* or *Voss* or *Bullocky* for the purposes of an examination might, nevertheless, continue to behave as if he agreed with the curriculum and its associated pedagogy in order that the parents of his students might not complain of the lack of success of his students in some external examination. Again, and in relation to the moral curriculum, parents have been known to object to teachers who taught what they saw as immoral behaviour, particularly in relation to sexual matters. Teachers in state schools in Australia have lost their jobs in such cases. These incidents serve to show teachers the limits of tolerable curricular behaviour and force those that disagree to conform.

Whether because of consensus or because of compliance or because of lack of competence to change things, curricular stability is not uncommon either within any one school or even within school subjects across systems. But the knowledge selected for transmission may in some ways not match the currently perceived needs of the society concerned. No assumption is being made here that the curriculum, according to some set of values, always ought to match social requirements, however they may be defined. But there are occasions when, for example, the amount, the type and the content of science taught in schools may all be deficient for the present operation of a society either because, for example, the economy needs more scientific workers or because the electorate fails to understand the scientific issues at stake in environmental or military policy. Again, the direction of the moral curriculum may be seen to be faulty in that loyalty to the regime may be lacking or too strongly entrenched, or citizens may be so selfish that the interests of the old, the young, women, Aborigines, or the unemployed or some other group, newly seen as deprived, may be forgotten.

When such changes occur the curriculum may be challenged. But all formal organisations, and schools or educational systems are no exception, tend to become rather rigid in their working. Indeed education, inasmuch as one of its major aims and functions is to transmit the existing stock of knowledge, is more prone than many organisations to conservatism. Though a capitalist economy thrives on change, its educational system, paradoxically, is dedicated in large measure to stability. Thus curricular lags are common and often bring about conflict amongst teachers, administrators and educationalists. The conflict may become so great that the lay public becomes involved. By the mid-1960s in many societies the public, or perhaps more accurately the politicians that the public had voted into power, had become so worried about the unequal chances for different social classes within the educational system that they voted for a large expansion in educational expenditure; a decade later the political fashion had changed and the cry was for accountability—curricular results should be measureable in some way so that wastage could be spotted and unwanted educational efforts could be eliminated. The point to be made is that ultimately, and despite political or other activities in opposition to the challenge to the *status quo*, the conflict may no longer be contained, and curricular change may ensue.

3. Change

When an educational crisis occurs, those who are involved in making decisions about curricula are faced with a set of social constraints within which change is possible, but for all the reasons outlined in the last section major change is difficult for them to achieve or even to envisage. There are three logical possibilities, each of which have been exemplified in history, though only two of these outcomes have so far been found in Australian history.

The most usual outcome is that under the pressure of challenge to the *status quo* those with power either allow or generate curricular change within the bounds of the present system. Present assumptions are not changed, though they may be extended or elaborated. Thus in the late 1950s, after the Russians launched Sputnik, first the Americans and then other Western societies considered very seriously what action should be taken to meet this challenge, as they defined it, pressing upon them from outside. The general response, in Australia eventually as elsewhere, was to elaborate their facilities for educating scientists by, for example, expanding the tertiary system, building new laboratories and replanning science curricula.

A more unusual response to crisis is a major reconstruction of the educational system—including the curriculum. All assumptions are questioned so that great change is possible. This reaction is usually reserved for a very severe crisis. Thus in 1806 Napoleon's armies totally defeated the Prussians at Jena. The previous success of Prussia, a country with few natural endowments, had been built upon its carefully planned use of the resources that it had, and especially upon its manpower. Education had, therefore, an important part to play in Prussian society, but military defeat was interpreted as societal failure and hence there was need for a total rethinking of the social framework—including the educational system. Under von Humboldt between 1809 and 1810 a major reconstruction was planned which led to the foundation of the University of Berlin and of a new Prussian secondary system. The influence of these developments upon the nineteenth century growth of Germany and upon tertiary educational development throughout the world was immense. Australia has had to face only one such situation—the defeat of the imperial forces in South-East Asia in 1942. This did not have major educational implications, although some industrial training schemes were necessary to provide man-power, and particular woman-power, for the now much more independent Australian war effort.

The third possibility is that no reaction at all occurs to meet the crisis. Thus in 1917 the defeat of Imperial Russia by Germany led to the gradual disintegration of the society as then known until a new and very different social structure was constructed by the Communists who eventually gained power. Because of political infighting no group amongst those formerly controlling Russia was strong enough to rally sufficient forces to regenerate the society immediately, in the way in which the Prussians did in the early nineteenth century. No such crisis has beset Australia as yet, although it could be the aim of some political parties to achieve such a situation.

Those who face educational crises of various dimensions have to act within a given social setting which constrains their future actions. They can either work within these settings, largely taking them for granted, or they can try to overcome these constraints and make their world anew. These educational settings can be analysed on two levels. Firstly, the social structure can be examined in order to discover which social institutions interlock closely with education and in order to try to calculate which institutions have most or least salience for education. Secondly, analysis can be undertaken of the ideologies held by those with power and by those challenging it in order to find out the nature of the beliefs, values and possible actions of those who are struggling for change or for stability. Something will now be said about each of these analytical levels.

i)   The Structural Setting. When sociologists speak of social institutions they are referring to partially bounded networks of social interaction centred on clusters of values which have come to be seen as important for the society under consideration. In our society, and in most similar societies, education is one such institution. There is a whole series of linked formal organisations—for example, schools, colleges, universities, and processes such as teaching, learning and apprenticeship, that are focused around the control and distribution of a society's stock of knowledge.

In the Australian social structure education is linked with a number of other institutions. Thus the family which focuses upon those values concerned with marriage, the getting an upbringing of the young and the care of the biologically related old, is clearly connected closely to education in that education depends on the family for support and the family relies upon education to teach its children much—particularly academic knowledge—that is beyond its competence. Other social institutions that are important for education in Australia are: the polity, which is responsible for governing the society and, therefore, controls the flow of resources to other institutions including education; religion, which is centred around values relating to ultimate things and which, therefore, is concerned with the control of moral knowledge; the military, which in our society has come to play a minor role and hence puts few demands upon education, though the suggestion in 1978 that a 'military university', Casey, be created could alter this situation.

Another institution of importance is the stratification system which focuses on values relating to hierarchy and deference. In Australia stratification is based upon social class, that is largely upon differences in economic position. In recent years the place of education in helping individuals to retain their social position or to move up the social hierarchy, has been given increasing attention. This increasing importance has, of course, been related to changes in the nature of the economy, which in a capitalist society is the central social institution and the one to which much further attention must now be given.

Societies vary in their institutional structure. Thus in what are often called primitive societies—though anthropologists have shown just how complex they really are—the institutional framework is very different from that in contemporary Australia. The family is the crucial institution and one would be conceptualising the society in a manner that took little account of social reality to speak of education as a social institution. Inasmuch as educational processes exist they are part of the family. Indeed much the same could, perhaps, be said of the polity in many such societies and even of the economy.

As societies grow more complex the polity becomes more important, since collecting taxes, gathering armies and stifling dissent all demand firm political action. However as the economy became more central in many European societies a form of economy now called capitalism was adopted. Since this was based upon the private ownership of property, the principle of *laissez-faire* was crucial, so that much of the central control and direction that had, under prior systems, been undertaken by the polity was left to the price mechanism, or, in Adam Smith's term, to 'the invisible hand' of the capitalist system. Capitalism has assumed various forms. Commercial capitalism depended upon trading rather than industralised activity and characterised the economies of late medieval Italy and sixteenth-century England. Capitalism may depend upon agricultural or industrial activity; thus in the nineteenth century Australia exemplified a mixture of commercial and agricultural capitalism. Fully industrialised capitalist systems are characteristic of the twentieth century and certainly since 1945 the Australian economy may best be described as an industrialised capitalist system.

In capitalist social structures the economy tends to be the salient institution, largely because under a truly *laissez-faire* regime all control, except such minimal political intervention as is necessary to provide defence and a legal system, would be automatically achieved through the invisible hand. However in most advanced industrialised societies, and certainly in Australia, quite substantial intervention to achieve political control has been necessary for a number of reasons. Most important, perhaps, and first in order of time, were the results of the switch from traditional to rational means of production, which had two side-effects: firstly, there was an increasing need both for highly educated scientific manpower and for workpeople educated to some standard of competence which the educational system did not seem able to produce of its own initiative; secondly, the growing emphasis on rationality led to a sceptical approach to one traditionally important social institution, religion, and the resultant doubting spirit was the cause of much unease and lack of human direction in industrial capitalist socieites.

Another change than can be attributed to the coming of industrialised capitalism did much to reduce the salience of the other major social institution of Western society, namely the family. Women of lowly status had always worked, but prior to industrialisation they had mostly worked within the family. Now they went to factories to earn a wage; the care and upbringing of their children became more difficult.

The lesser importance of both religion and the family meant that the structures that had originally given support to the majority of people were weaker or withdrawn. Many problems of welfare ensued. Some were of a material nature; who was now to care for the young, the aged, the sick, the unemployed and the mentally ill? Other problems related directly to this last category. Mental sickness of various types became more common. This tendency included cases apparently of a minor nature, for example, school or work phobia as well as phobias related to a more important general alienation from the social structure that might lead to suicide or serious crime.

For all these reasons those in power in advanced industrialised capitalist societies increasingly intervened in a politically directed manner in the workings of their societies. Welfare capitalism was born. The idea was that there should be a safety net into which the casualties of capitalism could fall and from which they might bounce back, recovered, into some niche in a social structure that was still largely directed by those in control of the economy. Many of the detailed processes inherent in welfare capitalism are essentially of an educational nature, particularly since social medicine now aims not merely to prevent physiological illness but also to check the development of mental illness. Therefore schools are now asked to help cure the problems of alienated youth, of family failures that end in broken marriages, of moral despair due to the lack of generally held religious beliefs and even, illogically, to assist in curing mass unemployment, the cause of which is deeply rooted in the present operation of the capitalist economic system itself. In brief, under welfare capitalism education is seen as even more central than it was under former versions of capitalism because it has been allocated not only the function of serving the labour force, but an additional function of social therapy, which relates crucially to the moral curriculum.

The changes in the social structure to which reference has been made may be generated within one society or they may be brought into a society as a result of changes in other societies. As the economy of the world has become more closely linked in the last two centuries, that is within the period of Australian modern history, individual societies have grown more sensitive to external change. This is especially the case for the former colonial societies. Yet many African societies are still deeply influenced by the way in which they developed under their former British or French masters. In the same way Australia is still in many ways under the influence of Britain. However as the economies of former colonial societies have developed, they have inevitably tended to be influenced by the wider world economy.

External political influence has also become more powerful as communications have improved. In this connection the influence is mainly at the ideological level. Political ideas born in Europe or in the United States of America travel very easily in the late twentieth century—either through print, radio or television, or in people's heads. In all cases where change is imported into a society it is vital to discover which groups are influenced by or reject external influences. If the aim is to discover the social factors at work on, for example, the curriculum, it becomes important to know the interest and the nature of those groups which have the power, be it latent or manifest, to mediate change from overseas. At this point in the argument we are moving towards a consideration of the influence of ideology upon social change.

ii)   Ideological Change. The term 'ideology' is used with a particular meaning in sociological analysis. It indicates a pattern of beliefs and ideas that some group uses to justify social behaviour or the way in which the social structure is organised. In this way we can speak of a political ideology of the left or of the right which its supporters use to justify their political actions, or of a managerial ideology which those running a factory call upon in their dealings with workers. Teachers can be said to hold educational ideologies in relation to what is to be taught and how this is to be achieved. More specifically, these could be termed curricular ideologies.

These ideologies ultimately come to rule behaviour in an unconscious way. Indeed they are not often consciously taught, but rather picked up from older members of the occupation, political party or social class concerned. Particularly in the case of such occupations as teaching or medicine a whole structure of values that govern occupational behaviour is learnt during the initial training period. It is difficult for persons in these occupations to change their ideologies after starting work in them because so much of their identity and their future has become invested in a given stance to life.

Thus in each institution there can be found an ideology or, more often, a number of competing ideologies. In a capitalist society those relating to the economy will be very important. Furthermore because the economy under *laissez-faire* assumes controlling functions of a political nature, political ideologies must also inevitably be involved. To some extent in each institution groups of specialists will emerge who think about, modify and suggest changes to the relevant ideologies. Priests fulfilled this function in the religious institution so central to traditional societies. Today we speak of intellectuals in the same connection. Their existence ensures that the realm of ideas tends to have a life of its own so that the ideas held by those commonly interacting in any institution may not be matched by those held by its intellectuals. This is particularly the case where intellectuals exist apart from the institutions about which they are thinking. Thus today many intellectuals work in the universities, part of the formal educational system, though their intellectual work relates to the economy or the polity. So-called advanced political or educational ideas may be born amongst these intellectuals, but not easily transmitted to the relevant institutions.

In addition to what may be called institutional intellectuals, in developed societies there often exists a group of intellectuals who ponder the problems of society as a whole. These may be called cultural intellectuals because they concern themselves with the state of not one institution, but with the interrelationships between the institutions in the social structure. In other words they examine various aspects of the total culture of the society. The exact social location of these cultural intellectuals has varied historically according to the society involved. Thus in continental European countries they have often been seen as 'free floating', that is basically unconnected with any of the institutional interest groups existing at the time. In Britain, however, such intellectuals have usually worked in the literary field or in politics and have hence been middle or upper class, often employed in education or by the mass media, and occasionally have even had quite strong links to the Government.

As Lesley Johnson[1] has shown, these intellectuals 'were accustomed to a position of influence and prestige in society'. She traces the way in which men like, for example, Matthew Arnold—poet, literary critic and school inspector—, William Morris—artist, socialist and entrepreneur—, F.R. Leavis—critic, editor and university teacher—, and Raymond Williams—novelist, university teacher, and socialist—, have over the last century defined their role so as to allow themselves 'to function close to the centre of power'. Throughout this period they all wrote about the state of the English culture and, since the curriculum can be seen as a selection from culture, they not surprisingly had strong views about what the school curriculum should contain in order either to conserve what they saw as good from the past or to move from a bad present to a better future.

There have as yet been few cultural intellectuals of this standing in Australia, but since this was formerly a colonial society we may expect to find some influence from such English cultural intellectuals at work on the Australian curriculum.

There is, then, the possibility that ideas will develop in one of the other social institutions in a society and ultimately have an impact on education. For example, political intellectuals may redefine social justice in such a way that education as now organised is seen to be unfair. Furthermore the institutional intellectuals within education itself may bring forward a new idea in such a way that the present way of teaching is felt to need to be changed; they may demand greater freedom for teachers and students in schools so strongly that change within education follows, though it is problematic how often such ideological change within education itself affects other social institutions. Perhaps more important is the possible role of cultural intellectuals, particularly those in English-speaking countries overseas, in shaping the occupational ideology of teachers—especially when in training.

1. L.R. Johnson, The Concept of Culture and the English Intellectual, 1850–1975, unpublished Ph.D. thesis, Monash University, 1976 (forthcoming Routledge & Kegan Paul: London).

4. Curricular Change

i) The Dimensions of Change. Thus far we have seen how the curriculum is constrained, firstly, by the social structure and the relative salience of the various social institutions in the society under consideration and, secondly, by growth, persistence and change in the ideas held by those with power in a society. When crises, whether seen structurally or ideologically, occur, their effects are felt through those who control schools or school systems. The curriculum, in consequence, may be reorganised and a new selection from the available stock of knowledge, academic or moral, may be constituted as the new curriculum to be offered to students. However, curriculum is a somewhat global concept and can be divided into a number of dimensions.

First of all we may ask what is socially regarded as academic or moral knowledge. It is relatively easy to see some of the more openly taught elements of moral knowledge. Thus children are encouraged not to physically assault each other or, more generally, to treat one another as human beings; deference to those with authority is emphasised; and, despite considerable recent changes, boys and girls are taught to behave towards the opposite sex in a somewhat different way from the way in which they treat the same sex.

The authority of academic knowledge is also to be respected. However not all academic knowledge is seen to be of equal worth. Plato and plutonium are more important than pins and bingo. A crucial set of questions follows: Who decides which knowledge is of most worth? How much power have those who make this decision to carry it into effect? And, finally, shall this set of knowledge be distributed equally to all the students in schools (S.J. Eggleston, 1977)? The most useful analysis, for our purposes, of these problems that has been developed to date is that of T.S. Kuhn (1972), based on the concept of paradigm.

Kuhn has shown how in the natural sciences there exist agreed paradigms of what are the important problems that a science can study, what are the accepted answers to these problems, and how new knowledge may be sought within the presently agreed 'normal science'. This analysis can be extended with care to other existing academic subjects (P.W. Musgrave, 1975), although the paradigms of the social sciences and humanities are much less settled. Indeed in Kuhn's terminology such disciplines are in the pre-paradigmatic stage, since there exist two or more conflicting paradigms. However in all disciplines and at all stages of the educational system students learn some version of the existing paradigms when they do such school subjects as Mathematics or English or Physics. In a somewhat similar way they learn the moral curriculum and know what they have to do to be seen as 'a good boy/girl'.

The academic knowledge to be learnt in school curricula is controlled by such paradigms, which are in their turn controlled by those with power in any particular discipline. Professors and lecturers in universities pass on to future schoolteachers the accepted paradigms in the subjects in which they specialise, and if the students do not exhibit what their teachers see as satisfactory knowledge they are failed in examinations or their research thesis is seen as heretical because it is outside the 'normal science'. Such agents of academic respectability also control what is published in academic journals, recommend new books to publishers, and, in general, police academic deviance.

The curriculum that universities and other tertiary level organisations offer tends to consist of a collection of subjects organised according to paradigms. A similar version of the curriculum has become accepted as the way in which school curricula—especially at secondary level —should be organised, though in primary schools a much greater degree of integration of what universities see as distinct and separate subjects has taken place. Even parents, partly perhaps owing to their own schooling, accept this principle of building up curricula from a collection of disparate subjects. Thus they object to experiments that integrate subjects, making such comments to their children as, 'When are you going to do some Maths, or History, or . . . ?'.

Because of the unsettled nature of subjects other than the natural sciences and Mathematics there are difficulties in applying the Kuhnian concept of paradigm to subjects other than the natural sciences, but there are even greater problems in using it in relation to the moral curriculum under contemporary circumstances. There has been a movement away from the situation in the nineteenth century when there could be said to be a fairly widely agreed unitary moral code to a situation where moral relativism allows pluralism to exist (P.W. Musgrave, 1978). Whereas until perhaps the 1930s a strong case could be made that the agents of moral respectability were the clergy, judges, headmasters and the gentry, today this is by no means the case, and one might well ask what part the mass media play in the determination of various moral codes.

Assuming that there are accepted paradigms in relation to the subjects that make up the academic curriculum, the next question to be faced is to whom should this knowledge be distributed. Historically a collection of knowledge has been made available to the élite different from that available to the masses. Even when, as a result of political pressure for a more egalitarian system, a wider distribution of knowledge has taken place, the principle used in organising this extension has been to replace an élite of birth with one of ability. The result has been the development of different curricula for those seen as requiring an academic or a non-academic emphasis. The former, aimed for the ablest children, is abstract, literary, individualistic and not easily related to the real world, whilst the latter is concrete, oral and immediately relevant to the student's life outside school. Two cultures have been created in the schools and are being maintained by this division which in itself in great part parallels cultures related to the social class system. This differentiation has become firmer because in many educational systems separate schools have been established to specialise in different curricula. Thus in Britain there are various types of secondary schools—grammar, technical, modern —or in some Australian States, high and technical. Even where common schools have been established streams are often, particularly in the later years, created within them to teach similarly differentiated curricula. In addition, even within these streams individual subjects are given differing status; the Classics used to have higher status than the other subjects and today the natural sciences are often granted more status than the social sciences. Subjects also have been predominantly taken either by boys or by girls with the result that the ruling differences in status between the sexes have rubbed off on to the subjects concerned. Furthermore the status of curricula becomes attached to schools, streams or other educational bodies. In this way universities have come to be granted higher status than colleges of advanced education.

So far the discussion has largely been concerned with how knowledge has been distributed amongst a given proportion of the young in any society, but this proportion varies through the world. Far more of the young complete secondary and tertiary education in the United States of America than in Europe. Thus social factors are at work to determine the coverage of the educational system. In the mid-nineteenth century literacy for all was seen as the main educational goal. In the mid-twentieth century secondary education for all became policy in many societies. Though nowhere has this goal yet been fully achieved the cry has begun of tertiary education for all.

A further dimension must now be considered. The decision may be made concerning what is to be taught and to whom this selection is to be made available. But, in addition, the order in which the curriculum is to be taught, what may be termed the pacing of knowledge, must be decided. Logical considerations will govern much of the pacing of the curriculum in Mathematics or in the natural sciences, but this is not the case in the humanities. Such questions can be asked as the following: Why is Chaucer's 'Prologue' usually studied before the other Canterbury Tales? Why are Molière's plays read before Racine's, or Shakespeare's comedies before his tragedies or historical plays? Or, finally, why do economists today study perfect competition before monopoly? Merely to pose these questions indicates that some process of social definition may be operating since there are no real logical constraints at work in the examples cited.

Pacing is often seen as constrained by such psychological factors as what a child with a given level of intelligence can understand, but even in many of these cases recent work has shown that social definitions are involved. Thus today many children who once would have been seen as educationally subnormal are now taught satisfactorily in ordinary classes and learn material that was once seen as beyond them.

The last dimension to be considered relates to the method to be used to teach the curriculum. Pedagogy is often seen as totally separate from content. To adopt such a view is, however, in error. Both the academic and the moral curriculum can be influenced by the methods used in the classroom. Certain cognitive processes can be taught by encouraging discovery learning. Students who learn Science in the traditional manner seem not to have the same attitude towards the authority of present knowledge as those who have learnt by discovery methods and who may both question more and have the skills to tackle the questions they pose. In addition, many moral lessons are learnt from the teaching methods used to transmit the academic curriculum. Thus academic streaming may teach lessons of deference, of who is to be treated as more important; rote learning may squash creativity in students and encourage them to be conforming in their behaviour to their teachers and in their attitude towards the authority of knowledge. Furthermore the overall style of the curriculum may carry moral lessons. A collection of separate and unconnected subjects may lead to a more divided, almost departmentalised, personality than would be developed by studying an integrated curriculum with resulting differences in social behaviour. With the latter curriculum the authority of the teacher and of knowledge may well be challenged more often than in the former case.

ii) Common Processes. As already noted there are major cultural differences between societies, but we must consider the possibility that there are some common processes at work within all or at least some types of society. As Karl Marx indicated, the process of industrialisation under capitalism has resulted in a social structure within which the economy is salient. For this reason cultures which are otherwise different have a powerful common set of economic forces working upon them. This is the situation in relation to Australia and its former mother country, Britain.

How much effect this similarity has must be investigated. Certainly, historically it seems to be true that an economic surplus has to be generated before any large-scale educational system can be established. As this surplus grows with economic development there is the possibility that an increasing proportion of it can be diverted into creating a more complex educational sector. In addition there is a tendency that the economic growth, originally the trigger for educational growth, will come to rely, both for further growth and even for the continuance of the present rate of operation, upon the size and nature of the output from the schools and other educational institutions. A demand for basic knowledge of the three R's and for increasing numbers of men and women who have various complex skills is born, so that education more and more comes to be seen as having aims that relate to citizens both as individuals and as members of the society.

This growing focus upon technology, science and rationality in the working of the economy as it becomes more industrialised, particularly in the capitalist form, has sometimes been summarised by tracing its effect upon the structure of the labour force. Thus, the labour force before industrialisation was mainly involved in what has been called primary employment, that is, in agriculture, fishing and the extractive industries. After industrialisation had begun, an increasing proportion became involved in manufacturing or secondary employment. As the output of the economy grew, a large proportion of the work-force was drawn into distribution and service industries or tertiary employment. Though there are methodological problems in attributing specific categories of employment to these three divisions, there are still some benefits in using such an analysis and in noting the ways in which other social institutions are affected by the gradual movement from a mainly primary labour force to a mainly secondary one, and eventually to a situation where perhaps the majority of those at work are in tertiary employment. Clearly, such a way of examining the changing nature of industrialisation may have advantages in trying to trace the way in which the economy influences education and, more particularly, how economic change affects the demands for various types of curriculum.

However these economic forces, common certainly to capitalist societies and in some measure to all industrialised societies, are mediated by different cultures. This mediation occurs through the political process. Decisions are taken between conflicting groups concerning how the economic surplus will be divided. In this process a proportion only of all that is available will go to education; there will be many other groups attempting to further their interests, for example, the military or the mass media—to use an old cliché, guns or butter? Furthermore not only will such a political process determine how much in total goes to education as a social institution, but, similarly, there will be interest groups at work to influence the division within the educational system itself. It is to this political process that we must now turn.

iii)   Political Conflict. Various groups or their representatives try to influence the allocation of resources to and within the educational system. These groups will relate to the various social institutions of the society concerned. For example, the existing political parties will want to promote their own points of view—conservative groups to preserve the educational and curricular *status quo* and radical groups to move towards, for example, greater fairness and wider opportunities for all. Economic interest groups in their turn will want to ensure a smooth flow of the various levels of manpower—highly educated scientists, managers loyal to the capitalist system and workpeople accepting their lot. According to the relative prominence of social institutions, other groups will attempt to influence the process. Thus in eighteenth century England the supply of clergy was seen to be important, whilst at the same time in Prussia there was considerable concern with the number and nature of recruits to the army. Clearly such a political process is concerned with both the academic and the moral curriculum.

Intellectuals will supply arguments to support the positions taken up by the conflicting interest groups. They will help to justify both stability and change. In addition, they may provide the ideas that lead in totally new directions. This is particularly likely if the society concerned is faced with some crisis such as war, defeat or a massive social change as, for example, rapid industrialisation. Many such crises are outside the control of any one society. The intellectuals concerned with the development of new ideas may relate solely to one social institution. In this way political intellectuals justify changes to voting procedures. But quite commonly institutional intellectuals are building on ideas generated by cultural intellectuals who may have an influence on many institutions. Thus the late nineteenth-century demand for fairness influenced the economy, the polity and education; likewise recently developed ideologies concerning both individualism and the position of women have been widely influential. These last two examples have affected education and, more specifically, as will be seen, the curricula of Australian schools.

Within education itself interest groups will be at work to influence the decisions about the division of the available resources and the nature of the expenditure made. The government in power will exert pressure to fulfil its promises to the electorate at the last election and devote more, perhaps, to the primary or to the technical sector rather than to other possible directions of educational expenditure. The administration will try to ensure efficiency and economy in the workings of the system since resources are not in limitless supply. Teachers will attempt, through their numerous groups—industrial and other—, to influence their salaries and conditions as well as the quality of their students' schooling. Parents, too, will be interested in the outcome of this political conflict. There are two additional points to note about their position. Firstly, they are not experts in the process in which they are politically interested, though this is not an unusual situation in democratic societies, but, secondly, they themselves can be in conflict concerning what role they are playing in the political struggle. For example, as voters they may be interested in keeping down their taxes, whereas as parents they may feel that more should be spent to benefit their children. Finally, today even the students concerned sometimes feel that they have enough power to make it worthwhile for them to try to influence the political process—more particularly as it affects what may be called the chalk-face.

This last case indicates very clearly how the interest groups involved in the political process can and do change through time. Analysis, whether academic or by those involved in the process itself, must give attention to trying to detect, not only the possible direction of ideological change, but also the likely sources of, and supporters for, such changes. As the balance of political power has altered over the last two centuries within Britain, an aristocratic system, that could almost be described in terms of great families at war, has given way to a complex plural system with interest groups based in social classes, social institutions and ideological differences. A version of this change has occurred in capitalist Australia. One of the main aims of the next three chapters must be to discuss how the changing nature of this political struggle has influenced education in Australia and, more specifically, the content of the curriculum.

iv) Stages. When analysing change the technique of dividing the process into stages has been found useful. Such stages are artificial aids to understanding. Those involved in the original historical events did not see events in this way, though, paradoxically, once an intellectual has developed an analysis of this type, those who undergo similar processes in the future will be influenced by the ideas of the stages that have been posited about past events. Karl Marx traced out one simplified analysis of the socio-historical process. In very brief terms he predicted that societies would proceed through the stages of slavery, serfdom, and capitalism to reach the ultimate destination of communism.

Usually academic analysis is totally based upon processes found in the past; Marx used broad historical trends, rooted in fundamental changes of economic structure, to predict the future. Clearly, where the economy is central, as in capitalist Australia, any analyst would be wise to check for the operation of such processes as have occurred in other similar societies. Two have already been mentioned: the shift in the labour force from primary to tertiary employment and the move from a simple, traditional to a scientific, rationally based economy. There is, however, one grave logical weakness in such analyses. Cultural differences may be so great that very different patterns may emerge. For example, the attempts to speed African and Asian colonial societies formerly ruled by Britain towards what many political scientists saw as the ultimate political stage of a Westminster-style democracy have obviously failed largely because of local cultural determinants. Yet the knowledge of patterns of growth and change found elsewhere, whether in very different or in rather similar societies, does give us some purchase on the problems of our own developing society in that we have some idea of how we may possibly look at what is happening. On the other hand, there is the immense difficulty, as already mentioned, in knowing whether merely by applying the analysis we are encouraging the predicted outcome or the hypothesised succession of stages.

Educational analyses by stages are rare. Certainly in industrialised societies, especially those that are democratic and capitalist, there has been a common pathway of change in the distribution of education —one that is clearly important for influencing curricular content. Though rarely specified in terms of stages, education has moved from the private provision of a traditional education to the élite alone, through a system whereby the working class was given a minimal education and the middle class a fuller, but still private and increasingly utilitarian, education, to a system which aims to distribute a free secondary schooling to all and a more or less free tertiary education to a slowly increasing proportion of the population. Clearly to examine education from the perspective of these stages there will be much attention given to the conflicts of the political process, but not necessarily much focus upon curricular issues.

There is, however, one set of stages relating to educational change which does direct analysis to the social determinants of the curriculum, though it was not originally developed for that purpose alone. Beeby, an educational administrator from New Zealand with extensive experience in the South-West Pacific, was interested in conceptualising the way in which changes in the educational systems of developing societies affected the quality of the education given. On the basis of his experience in small colonial societies he hypothesised four stages (C.E. Beeby, 1966). These were:

1)   The Dame School Stage: teachers had a very weak general education and were either poorly prepared or not trained at all for their work; the school curriculum was ill-defined and the emphasis in teaching was put upon mechanical methods and rote learning; there was no articulated educational system.

2)   The Stage of Formalism: teachers might have had some general education and some initial training; almost inevitably the curriculum was highly organised and those in control of the system saw 'one best method' of teaching which focussed on the school class as a whole.

3)   The Stage of Transition: teachers now might have secondary education and rather more initial training; since they, therefore, felt more secure in their position and were seen by those in control as more competent as teachers, a less formal curriculum was specified.

4)   The Stage of Meaning: in this final stage teachers are well educated and well prepared; the emphasis in learning is on the individual and the degree of external control on the teacher is diminished; the teacher is concerned with seeing that each child develops fully his understanding of the meaning of the curriculum.

If such stages can be shown to be a simplified representation of educational reality, particularly in societies outside the South-West Pacific, they could provide a very profitable way into the analysis of the social determinants involved in curricular change. Two authors provide evidence, and in both cases relating to Australia, to show that this is the case. Hughes (1969) has analysed the development of primary curricula in Tasmania over the last two centuries using this framework. Musgrave (1976) has shown that some aspects of the development of teacher education in Australia can be viewed through the use of these four stages.

However, and more important, in one small study Musgrave (1974) successfully used this mode of analysis to compare the present development of education in the mother country, Britain, and the two industrialised former colonies, Australia and New Zealand, with that in a number of such newly independent, developing Pacific societies as Malaysia, Papua New Guinea and Western Samoa. It would, therefore, seem worth bearing these stages in mind when examining the social determinants of the Australian school curriculum through time. The use of this framework must lead to a concern with both the political struggles involved with control of the educational system in all its aspects and with the actual curricular content that is taught in schools. Furthermore emphasis will inevitably have to be given to the academic and the moral dimensions of the curriculum as well as to the pedagogical methods recommended and used.

5. Conclusion

A set of concepts for the analysis of the problems involved in the way social forces have influenced the school curricula has been presented in this chapter. By means of these concepts, the questions posed at the end of the first chapter can be translated into more specific problems for research. Answers to these questions should lead us to a much fuller understanding of what is happening today to the manifest curriculum of Australian schools.

These questions, arranged in related sets, are:

i)   *Control.* What groups controlled the educational system, or any one school or group of schools? By what methods did they exercise their control? What ideologies did they serve in the political conflicts involved in decisions about the curriculum, whether academic or moral?

ii)   *Resource Allocation.* What influence did decisions about how much could be afforded for education have upon the curriculum? Did decisions about the distribution of this amount between sectors within the educational system influence curricula? Who took such decisions?

iii) Structural Setting. How have changes in the social structure influenced the institution of education? More specifically, how has the salience of various social institutions affected education? What was the source of such change—internal to or outside of Australia? Furthermore through what groups were these changes mediated to decisions about curricula?

iv) Ideological Setting. What part did intellectuals play in the process of curricular change? Were institutional or cultural intellectuals more important? Were the relevant intellectuals working in Australia or overseas?

v) Curricular Dimensions. Were there differences in the ways in which the academic and the moral curricula were decided? In addition, did social factors influence the curriculum differently along the differing dimensions of content, distribution, pacing and pedagogy?

In order to examine the complex political processes to which these questions direct us we shall apply the concepts introduced in this chapter and encapsulated in the five sets of questions above in the following manner. There will follow two chapters (3 and 4) analysing the developing academic curriculum of Australian schools. In the first the developments up to federation will be examined and in the second attention will be given to the changes occurring from 1901 until the present. The break at 1901 is governed by the hypothesis that educational systems in all the former colonies seemed to have begun the move from Beeby's Formal Stage into his Stage of Transition around 1900. In Chapter 5 the development of the moral curriculum will be traced during the whole period of modern Australian history. The socio-historical analysis involved in these three chapters will enable us, after considering curricular change at the level of the school in Chapter 6, to answer more or less fully in Chapter 7 the five groups of questions posed here and, finally, to attempt some reply to the crucial, and very practical, question: whither the Australian curriculum?

Bibliography

EGGLESTON, S.J. (1977): *The Sociology of the School Curriculum.* Routledge & Kegan Paul: London. An eclectic account of present theoretical views in this field; evidence mainly relates to British education.

40 Society and the Curriculum in Australia

MUSGRAVE, P.W. (1975): *Knowledge, Curriculum and Change*. Melbourne University Press: Melbourne. An account of the sociology of the academic curriculum.

—— (1978): *The Moral Curriculum*. Methuen: London. A sociological account of the current situation in moral education based largely on British evidence.

BEEBY, C.E. (1966): *The Quality of Education in Developing Countries*. Harvard University Press: Cambridge.

HUGHES, P.W. (1969): 'Changes in Primary Curriculum in Tasmania', *Australian Journal of Education* 13 (2), 130–46.

KUHN, T.S. (1972): *The Structure of Scientific Revolutions* 2nd enlarged ed. Chicago University Press: Chicago.

MUSGRAVE, P.W. (1974): 'Primary Schools, Teacher Training and Change: Beeby Reconsidered', *Papua and New Guinea Journal of Education* 10 (1), 42–47.

—— (1976): 'After Freedom, Whither Teacher Education?', in Murray-Smith, S., ed. *Melbourne Studies in Education 1976*. Melbourne University Press: Melbourne. pp. 188–208.

3. The Changing Australian Academic Curriculum to Federation

> But the outward organisation of this nascent form of education already reveals an essential peculiarity which characterises the whole system which followed it.
>
> (E. Durkheim, 1977: 26)

The period will for convenience be divided into the years before and after about 1870 because major administrative changes occurred in all colonies around that date. Within each of these periods we shall examine the social setting, the situation in relation to the control of education and the curriculum itself; the interaction of the first two factors in determining the third will also reveal something of the way resources were allocated within and to education. Under all three headings ideological issues will be considered.

1. The Period to the 1870s

i) The Social Setting. The history of modern Australia is usually dated from 1788, the date of the arrival of the first fleet. Those responsible for its dispatch from Britain had but one aim—the establishment of a penal colony. It was almost by chance that they founded a powerful modern nation. The process of establishing what soon became a number of penal settlements was initially a very slow one; the convicts under their military rulers gradually strengthened their hold on an initially inhospitable environment. For two or three decades mere subsistence was difficult enough, but then year by year the area of settlement was widened. The economy of the time was firmly based on agriculture, but, as the number of freedmen grew and as immigrants became more common, a market for commercial services was established. Agricultural necessities and even domestic luxuries were imported, whilst the produce of the land was exported. As yet, however, factories such as were then growing common in the industrial midlands and north of the mother country were unknown. Thus a few small workshops could meet most of the needs for agricultural implements and their repair.

The discovery of gold in the early 1850s gave a great boost to the economy—especially in Victoria and New South Wales. Melbourne and Sydney grew rapidly into large Victorian cities. The increased wealth strengthened their positions as entrepôts, but some of the new wealth began to be invested locally, both in such secondary industries as the manufacture of clothing and in meeting the increased needs for services in any large city.

Up to the 1820s the key social institution in the Australian social structure was, inevitably, the military regime, which, under the governor, ruled the scattered settlements. The increasing number of freedmen and the coming of substantial numbers of migrants who had never been either convicts or concerned with the penal system encouraged the change to a society more of the type that had been known in the mother country. The democratic background of the colonists reasserted itself, though the nature of their new environment, marked as it was by a geographical vastness and a need for individual initiative unknown in their tiny settled island homeland, almost inevitably meant that the political machinery ultimately devised would be somewhat different from that in Britain.

The ideological basis of those who ruled the convict society had been aristocratic and Anglican. The 1830s saw the beginning of great changes in Britain towards a more democratic style of government. The similar changes in the colonies had other and more local roots. Here men really were equal before the natural perils of the country as they struggled to tame a continent and develop a more settled agriculture. Furthermore although the colonists might believe in *laissez-faire* in strictly economic matters, they saw that the usual extension of this economic ideology, which would have allowed many decisions of a political nature to be left to the invisible hand, was impossible in Australia. Here, for example, the land supply was still controlled by the Government, so that the development of the area of settlement did not proceed in a totally uncontrolled fashion. In addition, slow communication, both to the ultimate seat of power, London, and within the colonies themselves, necessitated a greater concentration of political power. In such ways the colonists' democratic heritage was inevitably influenced by local conditions.

Early on, education was a matter to which little or no thought was given. Those responsible for founding a penal colony did not in the late eighteenth century see their enterprise as an educational one. Indeed they saw no need until the 1830s to make any statutory provision for the education of the working class of the mother country itself, and it was from this source that the majority of those transported were drawn. As the economy became stronger and a surplus above mere subsistence emerged, the establishment of schools became a possibility. Furthermore as the numbers of settlers with native-born children grew, the need for some schools was recognised. The contemporary colonial demand for education rested mainly upon three foundations, the nature of which can clearly be understood from a set of simple questions. In 1853 George Rusden, one of the founders of elementary education in both Victoria and New South Wales, asked, 'How shall the people understand the preacher, how shall they respect the laws, how shall they know what senator to support, if they are unable to think and to read?' (A.G. Austin and R.J.W. Selleck, 1975: 11). A population that had originally consisted mainly of convicts was not seen as a sound foundation for a moral society. Therefore the preservation of religion and of morality, then closely connected in most middle class people's mind with the practice of revealed religion, was essential. As a writer in the *Van Diemen's Land Monthly Magazine* perhaps rather luridly put it in 1835,

> Hordes of Boys annually landed here from the Parent Country with minds contaminated, and constitutions diseased, inured to deceit, falsehood and c rime! These are some of the elements of future population! It is with them the state must work.
>
> *(op. cit.:* 16)

If religion and morality were the first two concerns, 'making the State work' was the third. Democratic elections, it was felt, demanded an enlightened electorate who could read and write.

As the economy became more complex towards the latter part of this period and the proportion in secondary and tertiary employment grew, there was born a further demand for education. The switch in emphasis can be seen in a passage from the Tasmanian Royal Commission on Public Education of 1867,

> Hence Public Schools are now considered absolutely necessary alike to supply the labour market, to raise up industrious and intelligent artisans and tradesmen to assist in developing the natural and material wealth of a country, and for the maintenance of law and order in society.
>
> *(op. cit.:* 13)

An indication of the scale of the contemporary educational problem and of the present rate of growth in education can be seen in figures concerning literacy (percentages of total population in brackets) drawn from the *Official Yearbook of the Commonwealth of Australia* (1912):

	Cannot read	Read only	Read and Write	Total
1861	348,952 (30.3)	140,027(12.2)	662,212 (57.5)	1,151,191
1871	447,842 (26.9)	177,596(10.7)	1,037,601(62.4)	1,663,039

(*op.cit.*: 90)

Though there was some decline in illiteracy over this decade, the rate of the rise in the total population was so great as to increase enormously the need for educational provision.

ii)   Control. In the early days the colonies were rigidly controlled societies. Nothing of any importance could be done without the permission of the military rulers who in any case controlled most of the resources, even of manpower—namely the convicts. But as the area of settlement widened, the tradition of central control, or at least of much control from the centre, did not change rapidly despite the immense difficulties implicit in the close administration of a very scattered population without any means of rapid communication.

There were various reasons for this growing tradition of centralised control in Australia. Initially the colonies were expected to live off their own resources so that close control of the allocation of finance and resources seemed an inevitable procedure. As indicated above, religion and morals were also seen as items for the administrative agenda so that the obvious providers of education seemed to be, as in the mother country, the religious bodies, and particularly, perhaps, the established Anglican church. Therefore the issue of control of education had, by the 1830s, come to be focused on the manner in which the State would help or permit various religious bodies to provide schools. This was the situation in regard to schools for the working class. The middle class were expected, in *laissez-faire* fashion, to provide their own schooling so that a number of private adventure schools, often short lived, had begun to appear, over which the State exercised little or no control.

However in the 1840s in all colonies rapid growth, increased wealth and the changing nature of the social structure enabled the foundation of parallel or dual systems of education. Schools were provided under officially recognised bodies by both the State and the denominations. There were increasing problems in operating this system. These were largely political in nature, but were tied to the origins of the dual system in religious differences. Many believed that the answer was that the State should provide secular education. On the other hand, nonconformists, and particularly the Roman Catholics, wished to preserve their faith by the teaching of religion in schools, which, if the State would not finance, they themselves would both provide and control. The political problem in essence related to who would be allowed to provide the resources for education; the educational outcome was that, since he who paid the piper could call the tune, the curriculum would be different within the various types of schools provided.

During this period of political confusion schools of a sort were established, but their distribution over the colonies was most uneven. This in itself was an offence to the growing feeling in the colonies that inequalities between citizens should be avoided. Clearly, then, the dual system was developing schools in such a way that the result could be both divisive and inegalitarian. Both these results were contrary to the developing beliefs that were later to be fundamental to the myths upon which Australian society was to rest.

In essence, growing wealth and freedom had encouraged the demand for education for the working class, but the salience of religion as an institution, imported from the mother country, allowed much control over education to religious bodies, and the conditions peculiar to the rapidly growing colonies, especially after 1850, encouraged a continuance of central control.

iii)   Education. Elementary education in the early nineteenth century was provided very much on an *ad hoc* basis except in some of the penal institutions where, as at Port Arthur, there was a special settlement, the ruins of which can still be seen at Point Puer; here some schooling was provided for convict children. Thus it is not surprising that when Commissioner J.T. Bigge wrote his report on the colonies of New South Wales and Van Diemen's Land in the early 1820s, he recommended that competent teachers should be recruited from overseas and that two training schools should be established to introduce the English monitorial system. This method of running a school had much in common with the way factories were run at that time. A master taught fragments of information to monitors, often themselves little more than young pupils, who then went off to teach those for whom they were responsible. Monitors came and went; the almost blind led the nearly totally blind.

Little was done as a result of Bigge's report. It was 1839 before any statutory provision for education was made in Van Diemen's Land;

then Sir John Franklin, the Governor, established a Board of Education to control schools to which state aid was given. In 1841 six trained teachers were brought from Britain and placed in strategic positions throughout the island. Some curricular innovations were made so that something more than the bare three R's was taught. But the content of the newly introduced subjects—History, Nature Study and Drawing —was defined by the textbooks used, which were either those of the British and Foreign Society, a non-denominational Christian educational body, or those of the Irish National System, written specifically for use in state schools in Ireland.

In New South Wales conflict between religious bodies held up any statutory provision that was generally accepted until the late 1840s when a Board of National Education and a Denominational Schools Board were established. In the early 1850s these bodies issued statements of required syllabuses. However progress was slow because a high proportion of the teachers in the schools established were either totally untrained or inadequately trained. Geography was taught purely as a result of the accident that it was part of the Irish National System whose texts were much used and, although there was a beginning to writing textbooks for Australian conditions, the material used was often specifically written for use in the mother country.

The Board of Education in Van Diemen's Land also began gradually to define curricular content, the course generally embracing simple Reading, Writing and Arithmetic, a perfect familiarity with the Holy Scriptures being, in every case, a paramount object. But because of the poor quality of the teachers it was necessary to give detailed instructions for what should be taught at each level and how this should be done. For example, in the 1840s work for Spelling was divided in the following way:

1st Class—consisting of those learning the alphabet.
2nd Class—those learning words of two letters.
3rd Class—those learning words of three or four letters.
7th Class—those learning words of four syllables.
8th Class—are expected to spell any word.

(P.W. Hughes, 1969: 135)

By 1857 the curriculum in Tasmanian elementary schools was described as

Reading correctly easy Narratives.
Grammar—acquainted with parts of speech, parsing.
Writing from dictation—easy sentences.

Geography—acquainted with the Map of the World.
Etymology—Latin and Greek roots, English etymologies.
Arithmetic—numeration, long division, rule of three.
Writing from copy on slates.

(*op. cit.*: 136)

Furthermore the minimal curriculum was taught in a very mechanical manner and even by the end of the next decade in 1869 60 per cent of those attending school did not reach the standard of the third class and only 16 per cent passed it. A very similar situation was found in the elementary schools of the other colonies.

Secondary schools were very rare. Initially the children of the rulers were sent or taken back to Britain for their schooling since Australia was not seen as home by their parents. As the numbers of the native-born middle class rose, so the demand for what now would be called secondary schooling grew. At first such schools were modelled on similar schools in the mother country which were, in the early nineteenth century, largely classical in their curriculum. This was seen to be the content needed to educate members of a leisured ruling class. The problem was that no such social class formed an organic part of the contemporary Australian social structure. As soon as economic growth began beyond the subsistence level, those responsible were a struggling, striving pastoralist element or the members of an entrepreneurial embryonic urban middle class. To both wealth was all. There was no time for the Classics. Very soon the question was put: what is the use of the Classics? The Australian secondary curriculum was born of such a fundamentally utilitarian question.

In the 1840s a new type of school was begun in which the curriculum was much the same as the eighteenth century English dissenting academies. These schools were secondary in the level of their curricula and in the age of their students, and utilitarian in character as they had to sell their educational services to the up-and-coming social class —the nonconformist middle class in eighteenth-century England, but the commercial middle class in mid-nineteenth-century Australia. The study of classical languages gave place to work in English and French —both seen as useful for a future life in business. Monetary and economic success was felt to be assured in this way; at that time political power was not, in general, sought by this class.

However the traditional classical curriculum did not disappear without a fight. In 1852 the University of Sydney and in 1855 the University of Melbourne were founded. Both aimed to restore the

Classics to what professors drawn from the cultured mother land saw as their proper position; this was to be achieved through regulations concerning matriculation requirements. In 1854 the University of Melbourne demanded passes in Latin and Greek in their matriculation examination for entry, though the provision relating to Greek was very soon dropped and, indeed, Melbourne widened the range of acceptable subjects more quickly than Sydney, allowing English, History and Geography in 1855, and French and German in 1862.

The classical secondary curriculum depended for its continuance upon a world of privilege largely associated with an aristocracy and a wealthy established church. As indicated, this structural support did not exist in colonial society, though something akin to it might have been found amongst a few extremely wealthy pastoralists. However this latter group still largely contracted their children out of the local secondary schools. Thus, particularly after the gold rushes when colonial, as opposed to pastoralist, society grew wealthy in its own right, the commercial middle classes began to claim political power and to develop education in the utilitarian manner that seemed fitted to their specific needs (E.L. French, 1959). Very soon the matricula- tion examinations came to serve wider functions than those associated with the universities. Thus in 1871 the Melbourne examination, if passed in English, Arithmetic, and two other subjects, allowed entry to the public service.

By 1870, or the end of the period here under discussion, at the elementary level the schools were passing out of Beeby's Dame School Stage and their curricula were becoming somewhat formalised, largely to substitute for the almost total lack of training of the teachers concerned. Content was, however, minimal, and was often not really apt for colonial conditions since textbooks were rarely available that had been written specifically for local conditions. At the secondary level the particular characteristics of the Australian social structure were, however, such that the curriculum imported from the mother country quite quickly was challenged because it was not seen to be suitable for the utilitarian needs of the commercial middle class who were rapidly coming to political power as the colonies grew more wealthy. Because of the control of the universities over secondary curricula, content was more fully specified at this level than in the elementary schools. Yet although the standards of knowledge amongst teachers in the secondary schools might be higher than in the elementary schools, in both cases training, when found, was of a low standard and had often been undertaken outside Australia.

2. From the 1870s to 1901

i)   The Social Setting. During the last third of the nineteenth century there was an immense growth in the Australian population and, despite the continued growth of the numbers of those who could not read, by 1901 literacy rates had improved greatly over those reported earlier.This may be seen from the following figures, once again drawn from the *Official Yearbook of the Commonwealth of Australia* (1912):

	Cannot read	Read only	Read and Write	Total
1881	520,356 (23.2)	138,282 (6.1)	1,591,556 (70.7)	2,250,194
1891	671,183 (21.1)	108,870 (3.4)	2,394,339 (75.4)	3,174,392
1901	674,522 (17.9)	78,614 (2.1)	3,020,665 (80.0)	3,773,801

(A.G. Austin and R.J.W. Selleck, 1975: 90)

But, particularly early in the period, much of the literacy and illiteracy was still imported, as was so much else in the colonies. The metropolitan cities in each of the colonies, the seats of their governments, grew as entrepôts for their primary industries. Pastoralists exported wool and, after the Suez Canal was opened and freezer ships came, mutton; agriculturalists exported wheat, and the mining interests exported gold. Though this period is known to economic historians as the great depression, for the colonies it was a time of jerky, but solid, growth. In the cities, mainly but not entirely in the metropolitan areas, secondary industry grew. These years saw the beginning of the division of interest between rural and urban Australia despite the fact that the national myth was coming to be based on the former, not the latter.

It is important to note that there was the beginning of a very real Australian consciousness during this period. By about 1900 native-born Australians formed a majority of the population. Men came to see themselves not just as Victorians or Tasmanians, but also, or even firstly, as Australians. One index of this was the growth of an Australian literature. Men were now far enough away from the convict past to make it possible in 1874 for Marcus Clarke to write and for his publisher profitably to sell the book *For the Term of His Natural Life*. The *Bulletin* was started in 1880 and, with a circulation of 80,000 by 1890, functioned as a focus for much of the growth of Australian nationalism. The Heidelberg School of painters in the late 1880s could begin to interpret the landscape in a style that helped to influence how those who lived in Australia themselves perceived their surroundings. Australians were becoming self-consciously Australian, however much they remained loyal to 'home'.

Increasing economic wealth at a time of business difficulty aided the growth of working class consciousness. The myth of equality for all came to be accompanied by the other powerful Australian myth of a 'fair go' for all, especially in the face of authority. Not only did the workers of the newly founded secondary industries feel the need to ensure fairness by trade union activity, but also those who in most societies are most slowly organised, namely agricultural workers, felt the same course to be necessary. This gave a new dimension to the workings of the political system. Colonial legislatures dedicated to the interests of the pastoralists in the 1850s and to the commercial classes in the 1870s had, by the 1890s, felt the impact of Labor politics.

The early 1890s were marked by severe economic crises and this period saw two responses from the trade unions. Firstly, there were a number of severe strikes in both urban and rural areas. But, secondly, and in the long run more important, the supporters of working class interests took the decision to fight for representation in the democratically elected colonial parliaments. It was during these years that Labor members were first elected to parliaments.

The 1890s were decisive years. The old problem had been how to teach religion in the schools; this had been to a large extent achieved by the 1870s. But now there was a new difficulty, still to this day not entirely solved, namely when and how to deal with politics within the educational system. Religion was no longer so central a social institution, whilst people were becoming more concerned with political issues, which were increasingly polarised along the dimensions most visible in the cities, namely along the lines of social class. Education was now seen as a possible agent of unity, not merely in relation to religion, but also politically. The schools of a wealthier society, now coming to see itself as a nation, must help to create a people united despite religious and political differences.

ii)   Control. The colonial governments had, from their inauguration, been strong. Therefore despite the strength of the feeling against authority that came to be seen as very Australian and the support for a measure of *laissez-faire*, there was a long-standing framework within which the greater element of bureaucratic control necessary to administer a more complex society could be fitted. Local conditions, as already noted, conspired to assist the centralisation of government in the metropolitan city of each colony. The strong tradition of local government of the mother country was not imported into Australia.

In the very years during which the cities of Britain were developing the machinery of local government which enabled them to cope with the legacy of earlier industrialisation, the growing Australian country towns were losing more and more of their independence to the capital cities of each of the Australian colonies.

Thus for a number of reasons the control of the developing educational systems passed into the hands of those at the centre. Partly this was the solution adopted for the provision and control of other services; partly it built on what had gone before in the field of education; and partly a centralised system could, it was believed, most easily ensure that fairness in provision which was becoming an even more strongly held part of the Australian political ideology. This last view was important, since rural Australia, the area in which the myths of Australian culture were rooted, must have the same treatment as the more reachable and, for many educated people by then, the more attractive metropolitan areas.

For this reason when the educational systems of the colonies were restructured and put on the basis upon which they really still operate, the relevant Acts of the colonial parliaments created centralised Education Departments under ministers of the colonial governments and responsible to the parliament of each colony. For various reasons, perhaps still not fully understood, the unrest concerning the inefficiencies of the dual systems in each colony came to a head in the 1870s so that between 1872 and 1880 four States passed Education Acts (Victoria, 1872; South Australia, 1875; Queensland, 1875; New South Wales, 1880). The other two States followed within the period under consideration (Tasmania, 1885; Western Australia, 1893). It is worth noticing that similar Acts were passed for England and Wales in 1870 and Scotland in 1872. In some respects the mother country had a similar educational problem to solve, though the solutions adopted were not always the same. The colonial Acts are usually described as 'free, compulsory and secular'. In Britain elementary schools were initially neither entirely free nor compulsory and arrangements concerning the teaching of non-denominational Christianity in schools were possible.

In the colonies such elementary schooling as was given was free, but each State covered only the barest of essentials, that is the provision of a teacher and a schoolroom with the minimum of necessary equipment; books and paper were to be supplied by pupils or, more accurately, by their parents. The system was compulsory, though only over a minimal period, usually between about the ages of six and twelve. Finally, though the curriculum was to be secular, each colony made arrangements so that some religious teaching was possible. Thus, for example, in New South Wales and Western Australia general religious teaching, as distinguished from dogmatic or polemical theology, was allowed, whilst in Queensland and Victoria the school buildings could be used after regular school hours for religious teaching.

The prevailing economic climate of the time ensured that this minimal provision was made in as economical a manner as possible. It was for this reason that a very rigid form of control was adopted in some of the Australian colonies. This was known as the system of payment by results. This system had been devised in Britain around 1860 and put into action there from 1862. In the same year in a modified form the system was introduced into Victoria. After 1872, however, its severity was increased. Put simply, a varying proportion of each teacher's salary depended upon the success of his pupils in a yearly examination undertaken by an inspector of schools on a syllabus laid down in considerable detail by the centralised department from which the finance came. New South Wales and Queensland did not adopt this system, but they did give their inspectors great powers over the promotion of their teachers. It can be readily appreciated that such a system gave great power for control of school curricula throughout each Education Department's domain. The legacy of this system affected Australian education for many years and as late as 1954 a distinguished visiting educationalist from the United States of America, R.F. Butts, could still say of Australian education what was true of the last third of the nineteenth century when payment by results was strongest, namely that the assumption behind the Acts concerned to provide elementary schools was that 'a little education is good for all children, but much education is good only for a few'. This 'little' was laid down certainly in detail and yearly examination ensured that mechanical methods, themselves also often prescribed, were used to achieve the results needed.

Since secondary education was not common, a system of apprenticeship was used to provide trained teachers. They were recruited at about fourteen years of age from the elementary schools. They were then apprenticed to a practising teacher. This method of training was inherited from Britain where it had been put into operation in 1846. There were differences in its focus as originally planned, and even in the way in which it operated in Britain, from what became normal in the colonies. The original intention in Britain, and what in fact often was the case, was that the pupil-teacher would proceed after his apprenticeship to a Normal School, as training colleges were then known. However such schools were very rare in the colonies. Fourteen-year-olds were apprenticed, spent most of the hours of daylight in helping their master to prepare pupils, almost of the same age as themselves, for an examination upon which the master's salary depended, and their evenings supposedly in undergoing the equivalent of a secondary education at the hands of their master, himself often poorly equipped for such a task. The result was that the elementary schools were staffed cheaply, but by ill-educated and poorly trained teachers. Furthermore, and again unlike both the original intention and much of the operation of the pupil-teacher system in Britain, the employing authority, namely the Education Department, had complete control over its teaching force. The Department recruited the teacher; it trained him in the way and into the curriculum that it decided; it was responsible for the inspection that determined his salary and, finally, it posted him according to its perceptions of staffing needs.

Control was almost complete, but in the service of what ideas was it maintained? The universities of Sydney, Melbourne, Adelaide and Tasmania (established 1889) were still small and not very influential. None was involved in teacher education in any of the now accepted senses and, except in Adelaide after 1876, until the years 1892–4 when, for a brief period, a teachers college operated in Melbourne, there were no training colleges since the pupil-teacher system was seen as entirely adequate. Any educational ideas would then have to be generated within the Education Departments or imported from overseas into such Departments. The same was true of more general ideas that might relate to education. Teachers were closely controlled and given little room to allow innovatory ideas of any sort to influence their work. During this period those in charge in the Departments turned, as might have been expected, to Britain for their ideas. Yet all the influences then at work were not British, but the German and American ideas that did have any effect here came via Britain.

This was a period when in Europe there was much ferment in educational ideas. Views were changing on the place of Science and of Handwork in the curriculum and on how both these subjects should be taught. At a more fundamental level the previous work of Pestalozzi, Froebel and Herbart was being reinterpreted into an early version of what could now be called learning theory. Finally, an embryonic philosophy of education was being written, consideration being given to what place education should have both for the individual and for society and also to where the schools stood in relation to moral education. In Britain much of this thinking was taking place in training colleges, but, since these were not firmly established in Australia, there was no similar focus for easy diffusion of the new ideas here. Furthermore very few from the colonies could at that time go to Europe to learn about 'the New Education'; those that did come into contact with these ideas did so through reading and this usually meant through books written not by the original authors but by their interpreters. Thus 'the New Education' entered the Australian consciousness in a very bland form.

By the 1890s criticism of the way in which the state-provided educational systems were working was growing. There were a number of reasons for this. In part, the crisis associated with the severe economic depression acted to spark off criticism of many institutions normally unquestioned. But the growing feeling that federation and Australian nationhood were now not far away meant for many that a vital young nation ought to be better served. Criticisms came from many sources. Some influential politicians such as the Victorian, Deakin, later Prime Minister, were critical of contemporary public education. Some of those with business interests at least felt that more could be done by the schools to bring greater efficiency to the beleaguered economy. In addition, one or two university staff, for example, the philosopher Francis Anderson of Sydney, were strong in their condemnation of the low standards encouraged by the system of payment by results and the lowly standards of the teaching force. In 1901, in a public speech in Sydney, Professor Anderson told the New South Wales Teachers Association that the present teaching methods 'were stifling the life and stunting the growth of education in our schools'. Furthermore he went right to the root of the matter when he said, 'Above all, the men in charge of the administration have been trained within the system and are apparently unable to go beyond it. Their minds move within a closed circle'. One of the most famous critics was Frank Tate. During the early 1890s Tate was a young lecturer at the Melbourne Teachers College; after its temporary closure, whilst an inspector he wrote a series of critical articles in various Melbourne newspapers and in monthly journals about the need for educational reform, particularly in relation to the training of teachers.

The results of these criticisms in both Victoria and New South Wales were commissions of inquiry—the Fink Commission (1899–1901) in the former and the Knibbs–Turner Commission (1903–05) in New South Wales. As will be seen in the next chapter the reports of these commissions had effects throughout Australia, though their emphasis was much more upon administrative than pedagogical reform.

iii) Education. The educational systems that were run by the centralised and bureaucratic Education Departments were, despite the myths of equality and 'fair goes', fundamentally constrained by the influence of social class rather than by any purely educational ideas. Elementary education was for the working class; hence it was free and minimal. The curriculum consisted of little more than the elements of literacy, in those days defined also to cover numeracy. Secondary education was for the middle class and hence need not be provided by the State since the parents of recipients could afford to pay themselves, but unlike in Britain, where the classical curriculum was still basic at this level, Australian secondary schooling, though still giving much support to the teaching of Latin, had come to be marked by a strong feeling of utility.

The idealised elementary school in terms of which Education Departments tended to think was the one-teacher rural school. Its influence pervaded the system. The conditions and curriculum which could be taught there were those which on grounds of equality would be taught in the city school. The elementary school was supposed to diffuse a spirit of what Matthew Arnold—poet, literary critic and English school inspector—described as 'sweetness and light'. In his poem 'The Old Bark School' Henry Lawson gave a truer view:

And we learnt the world in scraps from some ancient dingy maps
  Long discarded by the public-schools in town;
And as nearly every book dated back to Captain Cook
  Our geography was somewhat upside-down.

It was 'in the book' and so—well, at that we'd let it go,
  For we never would believe that print could lie;
And we all learnt pretty soon that when school came out at noon
  'The sun is in the south part of the sky'.

And Ireland!—*that* was known from the coast-line to Athlone,
  But little of the land that gave us birth;
Save that Captain Cook was killed (and was very likely grilled)
  And 'our blacks are just the lowest race on earth'.

The drill and the rote learning, encouraged by the system of payment by results, and possibly the only style of teaching within the capability of the contemporary teaching force, led to mechanical knowledge, inert ideas and an unthinking product rather than a human who wanted and was able to determine his own future. The liberal education desired by Arnold was not the result of these schools, nor perhaps was the typical Australian whose real education inevitably was in the school of hard knocks.

In the typical Reading lesson one pupil read aloud, whilst the others, forty or fifty of them in a city school, followed with a finger so that they would 'know the place'. Writing implied calligraphy, and composition likewise meant grammar and parsing, in the service of which great literary works became mines for examples. The aim of the Arithmetic lessons was computational accuracy, which was achieved by incessant practice; some attention was also given to future personal needs, for example, the calculation of simple accounts; the subject was seen as 'useful mental discipline'. Geography and History were largely pure cramming of facts into already overburdened memories. Science was often taught without any practical work and without reference to local flora or fauna. Drawing and so-called practical work was inspected in the same way as the other subjects so that the spirit of drill affected them too. There was little room for either the reality or the joy of living outside the classroom in the curriculum of the late nineteenth century elementary school. Even organised games were slow to be taken up within the subject of Physical Education, which, of course, really meant drill.

Except in Queensland and New South Wales there were no state-provided secondary schools and even in these two States there were few such schools. The private secondary schools met the need for this type of schooling and their curriculum, much influenced by university matriculation requirements, was academic. These schools can be divided into two categories. There were, firstly, the schools that were to become the Great Public Schools of today, but, secondly, there were a large number of proprietary or adventure schools, many of which met the growing need for the education of girls. Recent work by Jagan on the Victorian secondary schools during this period from 1858 to 1880 has shown that what may be called the upper middle class mainly sent their children to the first category. About 45 per cent of the children of this class went through these schools and on to the Melbourne University, whilst about 40 per cent entered the public service. The lower middle class more often patronised the proprietary schools and a greater proportion of these children went into the public service.[1]

1. L. Jagan, Education and the Social Structure in Nineteenth Century Victoria, unpublished M.Ed. thesis in progress, Monash University, 1978.

By the end of the nineteenth century these schools were, therefore, even more firmly entrenched than previously as the preparation for a utilitarian life. Furthermore these vocational purposes were coming to be sanctioned not merely on the grounds of individual benefit, but in that they aided national efficiency at a time of economic difficulty and growing commercial competition—especially with Germany. Patriotism and selfishness combined to support the already strong utilitarian view of the curriculum.

Fortunately for those involved in education at this time there was, as is so often the case, a new theory to hand with which this new view could be justified. What is known as faculty psychology posited that the mind consisted of several faculties; there were, for example, reason, memory, attention and observation. Different subjects trained the faculties to varying degrees. Even if the Classics was now less often taught, much of its excellence for training the mind could still, it was claimed, be achieved through other languages such as French or German and, of course, through Mathematics. There had been some growth in the teaching of Science by 1900 and this development, utilitarian though it might be thought, could also be justified by the tenets of faculty psychology. Though the humanities, more especially the 'modern' members of this group of subjects, were still in a strong position in the secondary curriculum, they could now be justified with the help of this fashionable theory as useful subjects rather than on the former humanistic grounds, and this was a worthwhile ideological position in a society which had so utilitarian a view of education as that found in Australia.

3. Conclusion

The social structure had changed radically in the century since European settlement. What had been in essence the military government of a penal settlement had been replaced by a *laissez-faire* economy under the guidance of a polity with somewhat more directive power than ideally expected in a system justified by a liberal ideology. Secondary and even tertiary employment was now more common than primary employment. Religion, which was influential in the eighteenth and early nineteenth-century motherland, was still an important social institution, but a settlement had been achieved in regard to its relationship with education.

Fundamentally, the educational solution paralleled the social class structure that had been inherited from Britain, though the developing Australian culture was coming to focus around a central emphasis upon equality. Therefore, after the 1870s, a free, but minimal elementary education was available for the working class, though the system established to make this provision was controlled in a very detailed fashion from the centre in each colony and what little was done was achieved in as economical a manner as possible. The control of the curriculum was so detailed that there was little chance of new ideas developing within the system or being imported from outside or overseas. Secondary education, on the other hand, was mainly supplied for fees to meet the needs of those who could pay—the growing commercial middle class. Despite the control of the universities, the curriculum had come to have a utilitarian emphasis. The modern version of a humanities curriculum, however, could be justified by the new educational theory of faculty psychology.

Overall, second-class teachers taught second-hand knowledge. Despite high ideals the system was second rate and, by 1900, coming to be recognised as such. The era of the dame school was over, but in the manner in which the aim of mass literacy was first pursued in the Australian colonies a peculiarly dour form of the formal stage had been mediated by local social ambitions out of the ideas that had been almost entirely imported from the mother country.

Bibliography

FRENCH, E.L. (1959): 'The Humanities in Secondary Education', in Price, A.G., ed., *The Humanities in Australia*. Angus & Robertson: Sydney, pp. 34–55. A summary of a Melbourne doctorate which is the only full account of the development of the secondary curriculum in the nineteenth century.

HUGHES, P.W. (1969): 'Changes in the Primary Curriculum in Tasmania', *Australian Journal of Education* 13 (2), 130–46. An analysis using Beeby's stages of curricular change in one State.

Other References

AUSTIN, A.G. and SELLECK, R.J.W. (1975): *The Australian Government School 1830–1914*. Pitman: Carlton (Vic).

4. The Changing Australian Academic Curriculum Since 1901

> They could no longer be satisfied with the harsh and precarious existence which had characterised the beginning of their history; the rigour they had accumulated stood in need of wider horizons and larger aspirations, so that they could deploy it in freedom. The old structures were no longer able to contain this vital exuberance, were no longer able to maintain themselves; and this is why the educational ideal itself was necessarily to be revalued.
>
> (E. Durkheim, 1977: 173)

In this chapter the analysis of the development of the academic curriculum will be continued from the time of federation to the present day. Once again the period will be split into two parts with World War II forming the division. As will be seen, the economic and social conditions of Australia changed materially after 1945.

1. From 1901 to 1945

i) The Social Setting. Before 1901 the former Australian colonies had come to have a great deal of independence from Britain. Yet because of similar origins and similar environmental constraints they had also grown very like each other culturally. Indeed in relation to education the point has been made that the similarities in the colonies' educational systems were not due to interaction between themselves concerning educational problems, but to their independent imitation of the mother country (J. Lawry, 1972). Federation did give the Commonwealth of Australia independence and formally tranformed the individual colonies into States. The foundation of the Commonwealth in many ways did little more than recognise many pressures that were already at work. Therefore although inevitably, and especially in relation to administration and governmental structures, some changes occurred, the spirit of nationalism and the ideas underpinning the social structure continued as before, albeit confirmed in their Australian character.

The first decade of the twentieth century was one of much questioning in the mother country. No longer did it seem possible to predict the same imperial future for Britain as had been enjoyed during Queen Victoria's long reign. There were two immediate reasons for this feeling. The first was the rise of Germany as an economic competitor and as a major colonial power. The second was the recent hard fought Boer War in which an army that had been thought one of the greatest in the world had almost been defeated by what were seen to be a bunch of Dutch farmers.

Though twelve thousand miles from the European power struggles, Australia felt these same influences. Most obviously, German colonial expansion had come near to Australia's north in what later came to be known as New Guinea. In addition, Australian troops had been involved in the Boer War. The British response to these forces gave much attention to the place of education in meeting the German challenge. Hence it is no surprise that in Australia, too, education as a social institution was given greater prominence in the years immediately prior to the start of the war of 1914–18. For example, Frank Tate, the first Director of Victorian education, writing in 1908 of 'School-Power—an Imperial Necessity', could say,

> Germany has of late won many markets, and she has won them virtually in her schools. England has lost many markets, and she has lost them in her schools . . . All this concerns Australia greatly. So long as we share the undoubted benefits conferred by membership of the Empire, it is surely our duty to uphold it by developing at this end of the earth a sturdy, self-reliant race, able to work with brains and use to advantage the best results of the world's knowledge.
>
> (A.G. Austin and R.J.W. Selleck, 1975: 324)

The slogan heard often in Edwardian Britain, Education for national efficiency, was repeated in Australia, newly independent, but under leaders who perceived themselves firmly tied to the Empire.

The declaration of war against Germany and her allies in 1914 inevitably resulted in Australia's following Britain. Though there was much political conflict concerning conscription for overseas service, there was no real doubt that most Australians gave full support to the war effort. One of the paradoxes of Australian history is that her nationhood was immensely strengthened in this war in aid of the motherland, and more particularly at Gallipoli—one of the major defeats of the whole war. Yet, though both the feelings of nationhood and the ties to Britain were strengthened, this period saw the beginnings of the long-lasting problem of what the exact interrelationship between a free Australia and the mother country was to be, and this conflict had implications for the relationship between the polity and education in Australia. Many, particularly the middle class and the returned servicemen, saw 'Empire Day' as important. They felt that their 'British' view of patriotism should be encouraged in the schools. The political conflict between the Nationalists and Labor over conscription was in some measure transformed after the war into a division of opinion over what place the schools should have in encouraging loyalty.

Australia was increasingly becoming an urban nation. The percentage of the population living in the six capital cities grew from almost 37 in 1901 to 39 in 1914 and to just under 47 in 1933. Today about 60 per cent of the population is in the metropolitan areas. Since the population also increased substantially over these years the absolute effect was pronounced. Many of the contemporary changes in the Australian social structure can be seen in Table 4.1, the figures in which are drawn from the Commonwealth Census.

TABLE 4.1 *The Labour Force by Employment Category, 1901–71*

	1901 %	1911 %	1921 %	1933 %	1947 %	1954 %	1961 %	1966 %	1971 %
Primary	32.9	30.2	25.8	24.3	17.6	15.1	12.4	10.8	8.8
Secondary	16.8	19.8	21.2	19.0	27.6	28.0	27.5	27.6	23.2
Tertiary	50.3	50.0	53.0	56.7	54.8	56.9	60.1	61.6	68.0
Total	100.0	100.0	100.0	100.0	100.0	100.0	100.0	100.0	100.0
Total Labour Force (in thousands)	1.615	1.990	2.329	2.744	3.196	3.702	4.225	4.856	5.240

There was a slow decline in the proportion of the labour force on the land, though the greatest rate of decline did not occur until after World War II. Tertiary employment has always been high in Australia because of distances and the importance of entrepôt activities. But major shifts have occurred within the overall percentages quoted. Thus domestic service declined from 12.1 per cent in 1901 to 5.0 by 1961, though a very slight rise has taken place since then. However there was a balancing increase in the commercial and financial sector from 13.1 per cent in 1901 to 20.3 in 1966. Meanwhile, manufacturing industry was steadily increasing, except in the depressed years of the early thirties, though once again the greatest proportional rates of growth were found during and after World War II.

The reliance upon rational and scientific techniques in industry, as opposed to rule of thumb methods, was obviously increasing. Technological innovation also affected tertiary employment through such inventions as radio. Furthermore, even in the agricultural sector, science came to be given a higher priority. As a result the economy as a whole became more dependent upon research of various types. Clearly, scientific research would be important, but work in the behavioural sciences, including psychology, also came to be seen as worth while. Partly as a result of the 1914–18 war, and perhaps especially in the United States of America, much work had been done on tests for assessing intelligence and traits of personality and also on evaluating the outcomes of various types of teaching process. One outcome of this development was that, largely as a result of the visit in 1928 of J.E. Russell, Dean of Teachers College, Columbia University, on a grant from the Carnegie Foundation, the Australian Council for Educational Research (ACER) was founded in 1930. Tate, who had been a member of the committee recommending its establishment, was its first chairman (K.S. Cunningham, 1972).

The interwar years were not easy ones for Australia. Since the economy still rode largely on the sheep's back, world depression meant very low prices for wool and in turn seriously diminished all the incomes that underpinned other employment in the labour force. In line with the economic theories of the period, governmental policy was to reduce expenditure, thereby decreasing still further effective demand for goods and services. It was only in 1936 that J.M. (later Lord) Keynes wrote his book *Employment, Interest and Money*, which provided the theoretical basis for future full employment policies. The high unemployment did not, however, lead to any massive questioning of the political *status quo*. Indeed perhaps the new methods of rapid communication and the greater availability of various forms of mass media—radio, film, newspapers—allowed most Australians to realise that the whole of the capitalist world was in the same economic situation. Perspectives, even 'down under', were growing more international.

This last feeling, together with the increasing trust in rational thinking about education, allowed the ACER in 1937 to organise on a Commonwealth-wide basis the New Education Fellowship (NEF) Conference. A series of meetings were held throughout Australia which were addressed by a number of eminent educators from Europe and the United States of America and some other countries. The Conference occurred at a period when some political and ideological questioning had begun in Australia as a result of international events. Mussolini, who had ruled Italy since the 1920s, invaded Abyssinia in 1935. Hitler had come to power in Germany in 1933 and seemed to be bent on causing war in Europe. Finally, and nearer home, but affecting the mother country as well as Australia, Japan had invaded China and was pursuing a policy of expansion.

The NEF Conference did stimulate public interest and provoked much discussion, though it did not lead to very many major decisions about the educational problems of the times. New ideas were introduced from overseas and Australian deficiencies were noted. Reforms were demanded, but, largely because very soon, in 1939, World War II began, nothing much resulted. Once again in support of the imperial 'duty', about which Tate had written more than thirty years before, Australia declared war upon the mother country's enemies, though this second war was to have effects for Australia of a very different nature from those following from the 1914–18 war. A movement away from the British connection and a period of very rapid industrialisation began during World War II. The latter process was closely matched by the utilitarian view of education, which was as firmly held in the 1930s as it had been at federation.

The period between 1901 and 1939 was marked by the creation of a stronger central political apparatus to match the strengthening Australian national consciousness, but this process went alongside, and was probably confirmed by, the economic toils of the interwar years. Despite these changing structural saliences, the position of education had changed but little, as these words written towards the end of these years in the *Sydney Morning Herald* of 6 June 1930 show:

Most people are destined to earn their bread in vocations in which no great degree of book learning is required, and curricula which devote too much attention to purely cultural studies are apt to produce misfits discontented with their lot. In many countries, of late, there has been a reaction against the practice of 'over-educating' the rank and file, that is to say of equipping them, irrespective of their tendencies and aptitudes, with knowledge which is useless to them in after life and is quickly forgotten.

ii) Control. Federation confirmed and strengthened the democratic direction in which Australian society was moving. The new constitution divided up the various functions of government between the new State Governments and the Commonwealth Government. The agreed interpretation of the constitution during the years under consideration here was such that educational provision at every level from the elementary school to the university was to be made by the States. Each State took over the colonial system for the area concerned, but, as indicated at the end of the last chapter, there were major inquiries underway in the two most populous States concerning the reorganisation of the system that had been inherited.

Despite the democratic tradition and the emphasis of the administrative ideology upon fairness, the recommendations made by the Fink Commission for Victoria and the two Commissioners in New South Wales were still fundamentally based on the contemporary Australian class system. The Fink Report, for example, recommended that the elementary schools should be followed by continuation schools open to all and with curricula adjusted to meet local conditions and that the position of the present secondary schools should not be changed but that they should be for the few and lead to the university. This recommendation was accepted and it was only owing to the appointment of far-seeing and tough administrators in the various States that the provision of education, especially at the secondary level, was possible on a more liberal basis.

Between 1902 and 1906 each State appointed a new director of education. Two of these new men became very famous and were extraordinarily successful in rebuilding the systems for which they were responsible. Frank Tate (1902–28) was appointed in Victoria and Peter Board (1905–22) in New South Wales. Each was a former teacher and inspector from his own system, but, nevertheless, each had been very critical of what then passed for teaching in the elementary schools. Their achievements occurred within the centralised system then accepted in Australia. As Professor Anderson commented to a meeting of the British Association for the Advancement of Science in 1914,

> In the matter of education (Australia) has made up its mind that what it wants is system, and that centralisation is the best way to get it . . .
>
> (A.G. Austin and R.J.W. Selleck, 1975: 340)

In 1927 George Browne, later to become Professor of Education at the University of Melbourne, was to write, 'Under a weak direction, a centralised system would soon be a very sorry plight indeed' (A.R. Crane and W.G. Walker, 1957: 320). Fortunately, the men who were appointed to be the new directors were not weak and, furthermore, they were somewhat more influenced by 'the New Education', which certainly Tate and Board had met on recent trips to Europe, than those whom they succeeded.

There were two main organisational problems for solution at the time. These were the linking of what was coming to be seen as primary education to the slowly expanding secondary sector and, secondly, the inadequacies of technical education. In both cases the two directors viewed the problem very much through British eyes since both had seen the ways in which the mother country was setting about developing its educational system as a result of the English 1902 Act. In addition, they both knew of the way in which the equivalent public servant in Britain, Robert Morant, had issued a new Elementary Code and a new set of Regulations for Secondary Schools. Both documents were very much more liberal and less specifically directive than previous codes, and certainly than any such regulations then found in Australia.

Primary, or elementary as it was still usually known, education was, then, greatly influenced by what was happening in Britain. The influence on secondary schools from Britain was, however, less direct in that it was mediated largely through the universities and their entry requirements. Though a man such as Board was able to influence some aspects of the structure of secondary education, more particularly by building on what he had seen in Scotland, for example, by arranging that twelve should be the age at which students started secondary schooling, he was not able to do much to influence curricula because of the way in which the University of Sydney operated its matriculation requirements. The extreme example was Queensland where there was almost no change between 1919 and 1939 in the courses and examinations for the Junior and Senior Examinations. Some change occurred in Victoria, where a system was introduced in 1916 whereby schools could be accredited as Class A schools which were able to award Intermediate (year ten) and Leaving (year eleven) Certificates purely on their own internal examinations; the majority of independent and a number of high schools took advantage of this system. In 1933 an attempt was made in New South Wales to loosen the close control of the university, but despite a report in favour of change nothing was done, largely because of the opposition of the Chief Inspector. However in Tasmania in 1939, as part of a number of liberalising moves made as a result of the NEF Conference, control of the Intermediate Examination was removed from the hands of the university.

There were some developments in technical education in the period up to 1939, but mainly by its emphasis in a new type of higher elementary school. However an incident occurred in 1936 in connection with technical education that throws considerable light on the current views both of education and of its control. David Drummond, the Minister of Education in New South Wales, began a long and eventually unsuccessful attempt to gain Commonwealth support for technical education. The Ministers of some other States supported him for various reasons, for example, to give youths better chances of employment, to aid the defence effort as another war seemed to be near at hand, or, as Drummond himself believed, to increase industrial efficiency. However the Commonwealth stuck to the view that education was not its business, but was firmly on the States' agenda.

Those in power in Canberra were, however, probably strengthened in this view because at a time of severe economic depression a very cheese-paring view was taken of a function given so low a priority as education. The resultant close control meant that finance was very scarce, whether for staff or for materials. This economic view of education is seen very clearly in a statement made to the Institute of Inspectors, New South Wales, in 1928,

> Everything in connection with schools should be interchangeable like the parts of a Ford car . . ., and a child in 2A in Bombala should be put in 2A when he goes to Bourke.
>
> (W.F. Connell, 1970: 260)

The professional ideology of those controlling Australian education was not very different from that of the businessmen struggling with the slump. So curricular change proved hard to achieve. Indeed there was even educational regress in places. Thus in Victoria, although the University of Melbourne continued to provide facilities through which secondary teachers were trained, the Education Department itself withdrew from this activity at the height of the depression and had not restarted when war was declared in 1939. Indeed it was only in the immediate post-war years that such training began again under the auspices of the State.

In view of the quality of the teaching force in Australia, this was a serious step. Despite some improvements in the 1920s, by 1929 about half the teachers in New South Wales had not completed a two-year training (L.A. Mandelson, 1974), so that, especially in small rural schools, poorly qualified teachers were inevitably found in charge of schools. Though control was no longer by the old system of payment by results, and despite wide knowledge of overseas practice, which was now laxer in this respect, inspection was still crucial in all States and the promotion of teachers was tied to the success of their pupils as perceived by inspectors on their yearly visits. Sanctions were, therefore, very strong against teachers displaying initiative—especially against the known views of inspectors. There is much evidence to support the view that teachers were at this time a very conservative body in educational matters. Thus in 1937 the Queensland Teachers Union requested that the syllabus be printed as a structured work-book to show progress month by month—this, in the year of the NEF Conference. Following that conference, the Tasmanian Education Department initiated a number of important changes, one of which was the abolition of the award of skill marks by inspectors to teachers for promotion purposes. However the system was almost immediately reintroduced at the request of the Tasmanian Teachers Federation.

Attempts were made in several States from as early as 1914 to hand to teachers some slight control over curricular reorganisation. Consultation began in 1914 in New South Wales when the chief inspector asked for suggestions from the Teachers Association. In the South Australian Education Act of 1915 two teachers were put on to the new Curriculum Advisory Board. In 1921 an arrangement similar to that in New South Wales was made in Tasmania. Yet the problem was that such consultation could not go far or achieve much when teachers themselves were so thinly qualified and had not yet given much consideration to curricular theory.

There was, however, a beginning to the development of theory to meet local conditions. Textbooks were now published in Australia and written by Australians, largely by educationalists who had been overseas. Alexander Mackie, Professor of Education at the University of Sydney and Principal of Sydney Teachers College, edited *The Groundwork of Teaching* in 1919; in 1929 Christopher McRae, a pupil of Professor Nunn's in London, later to be the second Professor of Education at Sydney University, published *Psychology and Education;* P.R. Cole, in 1933, wrote *The Method and Technique of Teaching;* finally, G.S. Browne, later Professor of Education at Melbourne University, published many articles and two books toward the end of this period. The influence of Britain on all these authors was still very strong; particularly influential were the reports of the English Consultative Committee, under Sir Henry Hadow, on the adolescent (1926), the primary school (1931) and on the infant and nursery school (1933). The ideas of a more child-centred education found in these reports also came to Australia from the United States of America either through books, for example, Rugg and Shumaker's *The Child Centered School* (1928), or as a result of the visits to the United States of such men as G.S. Browne.

During the interwar years those controlling education, or their advisers, therefore, held somewhat more progressive educational ideologies than had been the case at federation. They might be categorised as eclectically child-centred, but they were still ahead of their political masters and the voters. They had to steer a difficult course between their own rather watered-down progressive ideas that were perceived as avant-garde by non-educationalists and the seemingly immoveable utilitarian conservatism of the average citizen. Child-centred education focused upon the individual, but contemporary national and international conditions forced some emphasis upon both the by now typically Australian concern with the vocational uses of schooling and also upon the possibility of achieving some social reconstruction through the schools. Martin Hansen, Tate's successor in Victoria, was in favour of moving in this last direction: education was to help to found a fuller democracy at home and a wider international understanding.

These social constraints meant that before the NEF Conference there was some reaction amongst the central administrators against their earlier apparent support for a greater emphasis upon the individual child. Teaching methods might be somewhat freer, but this was with the aim of increasing motivation amongst children so that the three R's were learnt more efficiently. As already indicated, there was no time between the NEF Conference and the outbreak of war for much real change to occur.

State control was as firm as ever after federation. Each State was in a position to go its own way, but common constraints of geography, of past history and of the common characteristics of the population meant that fundamental differences were few. This was especially the case because all States looked overseas for ideas and particularly, though perhaps decreasingly so, to Britain. Major change was, however, hardly possible in the 1930s because of the severity of the economic depression in Australia.

iii)   Education. Soon after federation the first major attempt to reconstruct one of the new States' educational system was made in Victoria as a result of the Fink Commission's Report (1901). The spirit underlying these changes was commonly found in all States and was deeply influenced by the contemporary social class structure. Perhaps an extended education should be made available to those in the elementary schools, that is in the main to the working class, but however this was achieved there was to be no interference with the present main method of providing secondary schooling, that is with the independent schools. There was some change in the elementary curriculum. Thus agricultural studies were introduced in higher forms and the content of some textbooks was revised, particularly by introducing Australian material. But the main weight of reform was pedagogical as, for example, in the beginning of the attempt to bring some reality into the schoolroom. Overall, the effect of reconstruction was greater and more efficiently organised inequality.

The first major reform was the ending of payment by results. Western Australia was first to make this change in 1894. Between 1904 and 1910 all the other States who had introduced it followed. A movement began away from the former extreme emphasis upon the three R's. Some conception of the effects of this system and of what schools were like in the early part of this century can be gained by a reading of Brian James's novel *The Advancement of Spencer Button* (1950). His account of the inspection of a District Inspector, named Mr Milling, of a New South Wales one-teacher rural school run by Mr Wren, is fiction, but certainly very near to much contemporary social reality.

> Fifth and Sixth Classes were having European Geography; the rest of the school were doing sums and writing. Mr. Wren said, 'The rivers that flow into the Rhine on its right bank—'
>
> 'Stop!' said Mr Milling, bouncing up from the table at which he had seated himself. 'Look at me—that numbskull who broke my bricken strap! Who can tell me what is—'
>
> The hands in the back rows shot up. This commendable promptness annoyed Mr. Milling greatly. 'Put down those hands, and listen, and wait. You don't know what I am going to ask you.'
>
> 'What *is* the right bank of a river?'
>
> Having been badly caught once, the back rows sat still.
>
> 'Ah!' Mr. Milling was greatly satisfied and beginning to enjoy himself. There followed ten minutes or so of hectoring, badgering, bullying and browbeating, but no one could tell 'exactly' what was

the right bank. In fact, the impression was being strongly created that the right bank was a mere myth, and that Mr. Wren was sadly deficient in having mentioned it at all.

For the first time Mr. Milling smiled. 'There!' he said to Mr. Wren. 'You see!' Mr. Wren saw all right in the midst of nebulous clouds of vengeance forming in his mind.

'Now, just carry on—' And Mr. Milling sat down again.

(p.17)

Less emphasis came to be given to the three R's. Art and Handwork were allowed into the curriculum yet in both cases the new subjects were seen as utilitarian in function. Certainly in Victoria Drawing, the main activity undertaken in Art, might be advocated as an elementary and basic form of art, but it was mainly valued for its possible vocational significance; Handwork, usually consisting of Needlework for girls and Woodwork for boys, was seen in much the same way.[1] Science was taught more frequently and in a way that aimed to bring reality into the school. Yet in all States, and perhaps rightly so, English was still the major study, taking about ten hours per week; Mathematics came second, receiving very little less time. In 1918 in all States more than half the total time allocation in the elementary schools was given to these two subjects.

In the New South Wales primary course of 1916 the aims and outline curriculum of the contemporary Australian school is set forth well in these words:

> . . . the pupil shall be able to read ordinary English intelligently, . . . express himself in clear and correct language, carry out the most common calculations of trade and business, . . . have acquired a degree of skill of hand that will assist him in the use of tools and training in moral and civic duties that will form a basis for future citizenship. In girls' schools the course will have been modified to admit of the acquisitions of knowledge and skill that will afterwards be useful in domestic and family pursuits.

(p.13)

One is reminded strongly of the English Newcastle Commission of 1861 which defined elementary education in terms of the ability to read 'a common narrative', to write 'a letter that shall be legible and intelligible', and to know 'enough of ciphering to make out, or to test

---

1. G. Hammond, Changes in Art Education Ideologies: Victoria 1860's to mid-1970's, unpublished Ph.D. thesis, Monash University, 1978.

the correctness of a common shop bill', together with a little Geography and the ability 'to follow the allusions and arguments of a plain Saxon sermon'. The mid-nineteenth century minimal curriculum for becoming a useful member of the Christian working class differed only in that it now prepared in a secular spirit for membership of the Australian working class.

There was one important restriction on radical innovation of a child-centred nature. This was the size of classes. Although there was some slight improvement in the 1920s it was not until the late 1930s that a major decrease became possible and then it was caused by the fall in birth rate in the depression rather than by any definite policy. However there were in the 1920s a number of important innovations, really pedagogical in character, but affecting the curriculum. Again, it should be noted that they either did not affect, or were applied so as not to affect, the core of the curriculum as it was then perceived —the three R's. Grouping within individual classes began so that more homogeneous sections of the class could be taught together. The Dalton plan was introduced from the United States of America via Britain; this was a way of individualising instruction whereby each child worked at his own rate on a programme arranged with the teacher. The establishment of special classes or schools for the mentally atypical was another organisational attempt to cope with individual differences, as was the establishment of a guidance branch by the New South Wales Department of Education during the 1930s. A further innovation with a similar intent was the introduction of free periods into the timetable, in which children could choose to do something of special interest to themselves.

A very important innovation came in the early 1930s when 'projects' began to be popular. This way of teaching had been applied in rural schools in South Australia and Queensland in the 1920s in the attempt to build up agricultural studies, but much was made of it, especially by G.S. Browne in Victoria in the early 1930s. The method had become more common in the United States of America and Browne had seen it in operation in Britain. In its original form the project was meant to be applicable to the whole process of learning so that children worked in an integrated manner, bringing many disciplines to bear on their central problem.If this type of project had been introduced the Australian primary school could have been revolutionised, but the project here assumed the form of a pedagogical technique to be applied within subjects—especially those outside the core of the three R's, and more particularly in Social Studies, as History and Geography were now coming to be known. There was, therefore, no radical reorganisation, merely some improvement of motivation in subjects outside the core.

In 1934 the Victorian Education Department issued a new elementary school syllabus. An enormous amount of work had gone into its preparation and G.S. Browne had taken a major part in this. He was much influenced by the English Hadow Report on the Primary School (1931). In 1932 a list of principles, based on Hadow, were issued to district groups for comments. Various trials were made in 1933, prior to the issue in 1934 of the new syllabus. In it American influence could also be traced; thus Dewey was cited. The central focus was, therefore, on child-centred learning. There was a stress on pupil activity and research by both the individual and groups so that the project was a very important method in this curriculum, though once again as a method, not as the focus for a total reorganisation of the school.

Browne was unfortunate in the timing of this revision, because it came at the worst period of the depression. Because of economies in the Education Department the details of the syllabuses had to be cut in size so that the number of the *Gazette* containing them was about one hundred pages; the syllabuses then in operation from the 1909 revision covered more than twice that number. This new curriculum made great demands on teachers that could only easily have been met if class sizes could have been reduced and if special in-service facilities had been made available for retraining. Neither of these possibilities was open to the Department in the depression so that formal methods either reasserted themselves or never disappeared. For example, even in the field of Social Studies, where integration was apparently widely recognized, the subjects of History, Geography and Civics still tended to be seen as separate and to be taught in their own right.

Educational theory was coming to exercise some influence upon curriculum development and pedagogy. Thought was being given to the nature of knowledge and its representation in texts. The 1934 Victorian syllabus showed this, although the revision in Western Australia in 1936 was even more influenced in this way. Scientific research on individual differences and standardised tests was now being undertaken in Australia within the universities, by ACER and by some state departments. All these trends were strengthened by the NEF Conference at which the visiting experts reiterated the contemporary overseas avant-garde educational prescription that schools should be child-centred, that integration of material should be undertaken, that co-operation in the classroom was more important than competition, and that internationalism was to be given more weight than nationalism.

Tasmania was the one State that was quickly influenced by the NEF Conference. Most external examinations were abolished. Promotion by age rather than examination results was introduced. Inspection was, at least temporarily, abolished. Handwork was taken out of the syllabus for grades one to four and the secondary curriculum was expanded to include, for example, Social Studies. The minimum legal age for leaving school was raised to sixteen, although by 1946 the applications for exemption from the need to stay till sixteen were at an all-time record and in practice the age of leaving was much the same as in the other States.

The Tasmanian reforms make an interesting case-study of several tendencies. Firstly, to be successful in a democratic country reforms cannot move too far ahead of those who are involved. The teachers wanted inspection and on their request the system was reinstated. Parents did not want their children to stay at school, particularly when it seemed to have no utilitarian value and whilst jobs were readily available in the labour force. Secondly, purely curricular change is easier of achievement than many organisational reforms because it impinges less upon most people with power, and parents, particularly, are not expert in the field. On the other hand, such change cannot proceed beyond the competence of the teachers who have to put the reforms into operation.

The one subject in which the contemporary tendencies might have been expected to have most effect was in Art. This subject, despite its perceived vocational significance, was never in the core of the three R's and was always seen to be something of a frill to the curriculum. Certainly child-centred methods could easily be applied in Art. There were some experiments in the 1930s but, except possibly in Western Australia, there was no major move towards adoption of such courses as were increasingly found in some Continental European countries in which the orientation was not towards applied technical skills, but towards the development of individual expression by each child. Nevertheless, certainly even in Victoria, most suspicious in this respect, 'terms such as "Art", "Handwork" and "Craft"began to supersede "Drawing" and "Manual Training".[2] In part, this slow taking up of contemporary influences on the teaching of Art may be traced to the

2. G. Hammond, *ibid*, p.41.

source of many of the tendencies in Victoria and, indeed, Australian curriculum at this time, namely the 1931 Hadow Report. In this there had been a compromise concerning Art in that both individual creativity and the technical skills seen to be socially desirable were given equal weight.

Two technological inventions had some influence in schools, namely the radio and the gramophone. The coming of radio in the 1920s was quickly seen to be of importance in a country the size of Australia where population was thinly dispersed over wide areas. Expert tuition in a number of fields could now be brought into all schools through the efforts of the Australian Broadcasting Commission (ABC), founded in 1932. G.S. Browne was again influential here as he had seen, and quickly appreciated, the significance for Australia of the early work of the British Broadcasting Corporation in this field. Between 1936 and 1939 the ABC introduced national broadcasts for schools and programmes for infants, co-ordinated their programmes with correspondence lessons provided by Departments for those who could not reach schools, and even began to experiment with the simultaneous showing of film-strips and radio broadcasts. In view of the comparative shortage of funds this rapid extension of broadcasting into the primary field was remarkable. It fulfilled two main functions. Firstly, some of the low quality of the teaching force was replaced by the availability of expertly produced material from the ABC; a good example of this was the introduction of programmes based on the Dalcroze methods of Music and Movement—few Australian teachers were trained to teach in this way. Secondly, in some fields reality could be introduced to the classroom; this was the case in some Social Studies work and, particularly in conjunction with the gramophone, in Music lessons where high quality performances were now easily available.

There were other methods through which reality could be brought back into the school. Science lessons were now more often pursued through practical work by the children themselves, and Nature Study, particularly in the local context, became more common. Another source was the use of visits to museums. In 1935–6, for instance, the Carnegie Corporation provided a grant to Australia for this specific purpose. As in Britain at the time, American funds, based ironically on past capitalist success, were substituted for the shortages caused by present capitalist failure.

In this connection one might have expected some efforts to improve technical education. David Drummond's attempts to draw the

Commonwealth into funding this sector, to which reference has been made, were a failure and little more was done towards expanding those technical schools that were in essence higher elementary schools with a technical bias. However one important point must be made about technical education at every level. Despite the strengthening Australian tradition of utilitarian education, curricula were rarely specific. The approach was through the fundamental principles of science or of applied art. This was probably because technical education had developed in this way in Britain from the middle of the nineteenth century. In 1913 a circular was issued by the English Board of Education which allowed and encouraged the growth of junior technical schools within the elementary system. These schools grew as low status providers of secondary education, teaching a general curriculum that had some relevance to local trades in that, for instance, examples in each specific subject taught were taken from the locality. The Australian counterpart grew in much the same way and, indeed, the problems for curricular development could have been great if such schools had been forced to keep up with every technological change as the rate of industrial change was, especially by the late 1930s, proving to be rapid.

The very fact that what was once commonly known as elementary education was now increasingly spoken of as primary education implied that attention had to be given to the links between the two fields, now seen as sequential steps, not as parallel systems with a narrow scholarship ladder from one to the other. There was some growth in state-provided secondary schools. These schools were seen as leading to the universities, teachers colleges or into professional employment, whilst the technical schools led to apprenticeships or, at the best, to employment as technicians. Therefore the new state high schools had curricula that were inevitably linked to the university matriculation requirements. These needs influenced not merely year twelve, but the years leading up to this final class because many subjects like Mathematics, the Sciences or Languages, are inevitably cumulative in their nature. Thus the lower examinations, usually at years ten and eleven, which were more closely linked to teachers college or professional employment than to university entry, also came to be deeply influenced by the requirements for matriculation to the university.

During the first decade of this century several of the new States made administrative arrangements so that they might provide secondary schools. In 1902 Queensland legalised the provision of state high schools in addition to the few state grammar schools that had been available since 1860. In 1905 New South Wales expanded its secondary system by establishing district schools with a modern secondary curriculum of English, Science and two foreign languages; technical and commercial subjects were introduced in 1911. In Victoria the system that had recently been extended under the influence of the Fink Commission's Report and under Tate's leadership was formalised in the Act of 1910 by which district high schools, agricultural high schools and junior technical schools were recognised. In Western Australia central schools were provided from 1909 (J. Lawry, 1972).

Thus at a time when the idea of secondary education for all was increasingly accepted there was the growth in Australia of the type of organisation that could now be called the common high school. This new secondary school can be compared with the traditional independent school. Therefore although in spirit the high school could become a comprehensive school for the whole of the youth of its catchment area, the inevitable result of history was that it was always in competition with the independent secondary school.

There was one noteworthy result of this competition between the state-provided secondary schools and the independent schools. This was that in several of the capital cities special high schools were established which culled all the high schools in the metropolitan area for bright students. In schools like Melbourne High School, especially, competent staff and extra facilities were provided so that the academic results earned would give that school, and through it the whole state system, the high status already possessed by the independent schools.

This competition had several other implications. Firstly, in many middle class residential areas no secondary provision was seen to be necessary because parents could themselves provide what they needed by opting out of the state system when they sent their children to private schools. Secondly, competition meant that the high schools did many things in the same way as the independent schools. This was crucial in the area of the curriculum since the Australian parent wanted utilitarian results from his child's secondary schooling. The high schools, then, came initially to have much the same curriculum as the independent schools despite the fact that a growing proportion of students were not destined to stay at school beyond the legal minimum school leaving age.

There were changes in the machinery controlling public examinations in both Victoria and New South Wales. These gave representation on the boards concerned to interested parties other than the universities. In New South Wales the Education Department, and in Victoria the independent schools and business interests, were represented. However none of these parties was yet really clear about the curricular needs of those leaving secondary school without attempting any public examination. The beliefs associated with faculty psychology still held sway and it was, therefore, not difficult to justify a utilitarian curriculum which would include, in addition to the core of the three R's, some relevant Handwork, Physical Education and Social Studies. The same general faculties that were trained in the subjects of higher status that were oriented towards examination were here exercised for the less able who would inevitably enter low-status occupations at the age of fourteen or fifteen.

Certainly the growing spirit of egalitarianism forced a gradual widening of the chances of entering higher secondary education. In 1933 Victoria abolished the external qualifying examination, allowing easier movement from primary to secondary schools, and in 1938 similar arrangements were made in New South Wales and Tasmania. Furthermore in the early 1940s there was a start to the abolition of fees in high schools. But despite the growing proportion of non-matriculating secondary students by World War II, the high schools were definitely still seen as preparatory to the universities or to the higher levels of the labour force and the primary schools, in their turn, preparatory to the secondary schools. The system was at least becoming well articulated even if the direction in which it was aimed was less and less fitted for the majority of its students.

The new educational ideas which had come into Australia in the early 1920s, and had seemed likely to shift the schools from their rigid formalism, foundered in the state schools in the difficult years of the depression. Likewise hopes born at the NEF Conference were soon lost when war was declared in 1939. However outside the state system and the traditional independent schools there were a number of so-called 'progressive' schools, most of which, however, despite some local fame, did not last long. These schools were nearly all private and hence had to survive off fees. In Britain at that time there were enough middle class parents dissatisfied with traditional secondary schools to be willing to support such deviant schools. This was not yet really the case in Australia. Yet from 1918 for a number of years the Theosophists ran several schools in or near Sydney. In 1932 Miss Margaret Lyttle founded Preshil in Melbourne under the influence of Homer Lane, an American, whose school she had seen in Britain;

Preshil still exists and, indeed, has recently extended into the secondary field. From 1939 to 1946 the Nields ran the Koornung School at Warrandyte (Victoria), a school much influenced by A.S. Neill's Summerhill (K.Cunningham, 1972). There was one progressive school within the state system of New South Wales at Brighton-le-Sands; this had been inaugurated by Board in 1917 and lasted until 1926 in its progressive form, though increasingly towards the end of the period its emphasis on Manual Work, individual choice for pupils and self-government tended to give way to the demands of traditionally minded inspectors and parents who, above all, wanted success in the Qualifying Certificate at a time when class sizes were increasing due to population growth in the nearby Sydney suburbs.

In the few progressive schools that existed the ideology of individual development was central. In the general run of state schools, primary or secondary, curricula were, on the whole, still very traditional. The stock of knowledge to be transmitted was still much the same as it had been at the turn of the century though its distribution was a little wider. Mandelson (1974: 85a) has summed up curricular development during the period as follows: 'the only generalisation possible is that between 1919 and 1939 the primary school studies became variously more child-centred, socially centered and more subject-centered.' True as this rather amorphous generalisation may be, the 'progressive' elements in the curriculum, more often found at primary level than at secondary, were usually put to the service of more efficient teaching of the core of the three R's deemed essential because of its vocational utility. What, following Beeby, we may term 'formalism' was not quite so strong in 1939 as in 1901 and this could be the case largely because the teachers were somewhat more competent to cope on their own without detailed syllabuses to follow. There were more teachers who had been trained and this did not mean so much that they were pedagogically more competent than under the pupil-teacher system— possibly the reverse, but rather that they now had sufficient secondary education upon which to build the beginnings of a tertiary education, so that they moved more easily in the world of learning. They, therefore, had more confidence to face their pupils as individuals developing in different directions; they no longer had to accept the role of a forceful shepherd driving each member of the large flock in their care over the same fences nearly at the same time. The transition from Beeby's Formal stage towards that of Meaning could be said to be under way despite two world wars and a severe economic depression.

2. From 1945

i) The Social Setting. World War II had two major results for Australia. Firstly, she had to face the Japanese war effort in the Pacific initially very much on her own. After the defeats in Hong Kong and Singapore Britain withdrew her major effort in the East to the defence of India. Australia came to rely more on the United States of America. This was a major switch in emotional focus and its effects are still being worked out. Secondly, because the Australian war effort became much more independent of Britain, a larger industrial base for making war had to be created within Australia. This expansion of secondary industry can be gauged in Table 4.1 (p.00); it can be seen that the percentage of the labour force employed in manufacturing industry, which had been 21.2 in 1921 and 19.0 in the depths of the depression in 1933, rose to 27.6 in 1947 and 28.0 in 1954. This change occurred within a labour force that rose from 2.3 million in 1921 to 3.7 million in 1954.

The years of industrial expansion lasted almost without break up to the early 1970s. During this whole period another major change was occurring to the labour force. The percentage of the population employed in the primary sector was almost halved between 1947 and 1971; the relevant percentage dropped from 17.6 to 8.8 in these years and it must be remembered that the last figure includes many of those working in the greatly expanded mining sector. At the same time, the expansion in manufacturing did not take up the whole of the slack created as rural employment declined. Between 1947 and 1971 the tertiary sector grew from 54.8 to 63.9 per cent of total employment. In this latter connection one other change is worthy of note, namely the increasing proportion of women in the labour force. In 1947 the percentage of women in the labour force was 22.9, whereas by 1966 it had become 24.9, of whom just under half were at work in the wholesale and retail trades or in community services; this relatively small proportionate increase occurred during years when over a million persons joined the labour force. Furthermore whereas in 1947 the percentage of the women in the labour force who were married had been 19.8, this figure had risen to 51.0 by 1966.

Under these circumstances the economy came to have a different importance for education. Whereas the schools at the turn of the century had been seen as the source of willing, but not highly educated labour, now there was a growing need for skills and competences at various levels that could cope with an increasingly scientific stock of capital equipment. Full employment lasted through the late war years until the early 1970s, so that the economic climate was totally different from the interwar years. Growth and confidence supported a huge demand for labour of all kinds. This was met partly by the greater employment of women and, particularly in view of the huge rise in the proportion of married women at work, there was a tendency to shift some of the educational functions of the family to the school.

However, owing both to natural increase and to a massive immigration policy, the population rose from around eight million at the end of the war to around fourteen million today. Increased immigration had a number of important effects. Firstly, as the numbers of British stock who were willing to leave the mother country fell, migrants had to be sought elsewhere and the proportion of migrants of Mediterranean stock rose considerably. Australia became more of a melting pot of nations at a time when there were already strong forces at work to loosen her ties with the mother country. Secondly, although some of the migrants initially brought skills, thereby saving Australian investment in education, especially in the fields of technical and higher education, yet their coming stored up future problems for the schools in that their children would increase the demands upon Australian schools, not only because more places would be needed, but also because many of these migrant children did not speak good English.

A much more varied stock of ideas was now available to Australia. These did not only come from the travels overseas of members of the armed services or from the migrants who increasingly came from cultures other than Anglo-Saxon. New ideas flowed more easily also because of the great increase in the ease of travel. 'The trip' to Europe, mainly to Britain, was increasingly a part of the life pattern of the lower middle and even the upper working class youth. When to travel twelve thousand miles meant twenty-four hours in a plane and six weeks' wages, insularity tended to wane.

During the early part of this period there was no real dissatisfaction with the political structure in Australia. The long period of full employment and the prosperity of the Menzies years bred support for a continuance of things as they were since this seemed to give good results. Thus despite the growing salience of education and the new dimensions of its importance there was no great pressure until the mid-1960s for great change. By then the situation was that the States could not really provide the funds to expand the system to meet the new demands put upon it, but the constitution was still interpreted in a way that defined education as entirely in the hands of the States. The Commonwealth, therefore, largely kept aloof from education.

Eventually, therefore, there was a concatenation of political circumstances which, although not a revolutionary crisis, was still such that major structural changes were possible. Around 1970 the economic expansion slowed at a time when the conservative parties ruling the country had embroiled it in an American inspired war in Vietnam. By this time the numbers of 'new professionals', mainly persons of middle class status largely employed in the tertiary sector, had become very great. This part of the middle class was not so deeply rooted in the existing social structure as were members of the traditional professions. They criticised the Australian involvement in the war and also many of the results of conservative economic policy. For example, the economic hiccup around 1970 led to the rediscovery of poverty in Australia, and concern over Vietnam aroused the conscience of many about the Aborigines, representatives of the third world within Australia.

For this sort of reason very many who would earlier have been seen as staunch supporters of the *status quo* switched political sides. In the late 1960s they did so, or were thought likely to do so, in great enough numbers to force the conservatives to reinterpret their view of the constitution so as to begin to finance tertiary education from Canberra. Small amounts of federal funds were also applied to secondary education. But the major changes in federal financing to education and to such other functions as social and community services came after the return of Labor under Whitlam between 1972 and 1975.

The new middle classes, particularly the professionals, had been somewhat influenced by a number of ideological tendencies, usually associated with more radical groups. Primarily, the individual came to be seen as of more importance than the society of which he was a member. Therefore equality was reinterpreted not merely to mean that the same chances should be given to all, but that an equal chance should be available to all to develop differently and to the full, whatever individual talents he or she might have. Finally, since the organisations that the Government provided were for individuals they, or in the vague word often used, 'the community', should have a major say in how provision was made. Supporters of such an ideology were vociferous in the universities around 1970 and the new emphasis upon the inviolability of the individual and upon the need for participation by the community was strong then and later in the policies of the two Whitlam Governments. Such views had clear implications for education. Indeed, the growing popularity of such views on education can be seen in the fact that from the early 1970s, the Melbourne newspaper the *Age* ran a weekly education page, oddly enough only in school term time, and the nation-wide *Australian* ran a regular weekly column on education; both papers have basically a middle class circulation.

Thus since the end of World War II the economy has had a major salience for education. Initially, under boom conditions, the results were a demand for educated and trained labour, provided at home or from abroad, within a stable political system and from a somewhat less prominent family system. It should, however, be noted that, ever since 1945, the position of both the family and religion has received support from the growing numbers of working class Mediterranean migrants, of both Roman Catholic and Greek Orthodox backgrounds. Once the boom slackened the political *status quo* was questioned, often quite violently, but eventually with the result that education began to be seen to be on the Commonwealth's as well as the States' agenda. A measure of the new importance given to education was that in a poll run by the *Age* just before the Labor Government took office in December, 1972, 31 per cent of respondents put education as the most important issue in the election; 37 per cent of intending Labor voters, compared with 24 per cent of intending Liberal voters, held this view.

(ii)   Control. Since Australia was, on the whole, so stable politically from 1945 to 1965, the definitions of education and of how it should be controlled, held by those with power in both the States and in Canberra, changed but little. Schooling was still seen in terms of provision by the States of a narrow, but slowly widening meritocratic ladder which led through the secondary to tertiary levels; at both school levels, a rather utilitarian curriculum was offered, under the close supervision of those who provided the finance.

This situation did not allow of any change in the way that education, whether in the primary or the secondary schools, was seen as compulsory and secular. Certainly, there has been little argument about the compulsory nature of education until very recently. However with the growing importance attributed to the individual, it has sometimes been argued that, since there is so little agreement about what the compulsory curriculum of a school should be, students and parents should have the right to opt out if they so wish, particularly where there are adequate facilities for them to begin their schooling again in later life (F.J. Hunt; 1972).

That a certain amount of educational provision should be free has also rarely been challenged, but what has been at issue is how much should be free. The American visitor R.F. Butts (1955) was very surprised, when visiting Australia in 1954, to find that school libraries were not wholly provided by Education Departments, but partly by parents and other interested local inhabitants. In the 1960s the Commonwealth Government, largely as a vote-catching policy, introduced the practice of providing funds for libraries and laboratories to schools, whether state or private. Gradually, more facilities have been made available to schools so that 'free' education now means much more nearly what it has meant in Britain and the United States of America for half a century.

The secular nature of schools has also changed a little since 1939. In 1940 South Australia permitted half an hour per week of denominational instruction to the children of any denomination that wished to provide it and in 1950 Victoria allowed controlled denominational teaching. Furthermore during the last decade, several States, including Victoria, Tasmania and South Australia, have all held official inquiries into the problem of religious instruction in schools, though without as yet any major change resulting. It seems, however, that the lesser significance of religion as a social institution has allowed the various denominations to reassert their claims. This has not caused the furore that such claims aroused in the last century, but the odd thing is that parents, by and large, would appear not to support religious instruction with the old aim of encouraging belief in revealed religion, but rather as an important source of a firm moral code to steer contemporary teenagers through the dangers of what is seen as a more permissive society.

More will be said of such moral education in the next chapter. Australian voters, often parents, and the politicians who control the provision of schooling, still view the educational system, more complex though it may be, as primarily dedicated to what Butts called 'the efficient expression of information' (R.F. Butts, 1955: 50). In the early part of this period, curricula were constructed centrally under busy administrators, largely as a part-time activity in consultation with inspectors, teachers and lecturers from colleges or universities. These experts had now more often travelled overseas and had undergone some form of higher education which had specific relevance to their professional work. There was an increase in postgraduate work in education in the universities so that the administrative controllers, if not their political masters, now had greater expertise.

Furthermore throughout the post-war period the quality of the teaching force did improve. This was a very slow process because of the immense demand for education due both to the rise in population and to the increasing proportion of students staying at school beyond the minimum legal school leaving age. Gradually, therefore, there was the possibility of giving more freedom to teachers to develop their own curricula to meet the needs for their own interests or style of teaching and the needs of their students. The loosening of curricular control probably came first, developed most rapidly and went furthest in Victorian secondary schools, where, in 1966, R.A. Reed, the Director of Secondary Education, began a process of consultation to establish principles, common to all schools, in service of which each school could establish a curriculum meetings its own needs. For some the process went too far, and often this was seen to be the case in relation to some aspects of the curriculum in Social Studies. Parents or groups representing other interests also objected to suggested new syllabuses relating, for example, to sex education in a Biology course developed by the Australian Science Education Project (ASEP) in the early 1970s, and in 1978 the Queensland Government forbade the use in their schools of all materials on social education, which had been developed as part of an Australia-wide project under the aegis of the Curriculum Development Centre, a body to which reference will be made later. Not infrequently the behaviour of radical students around 1970 was attributed to lax curricula in the secondary schools.

As various sectors in Australian society came to view education as more important, whether on the one hand, to preserve the *status quo,* or on the other, to change it by, for example, developing individuality or, again, to meet the challenge of an increasingly technological industry, so pressure groups were established, each aiming to influence educational development along the lines that they saw as best for themselves. Federations of parents pressed for greater expenditure—though often, as taxpayers, they voted for a party who would keep taxation down. Industrial groups criticised teachers because, they said, youths leaving school did not know how to read or add up. Ethnic groups fought for better facilities for language teaching in schools. Supporters of independent schools worked within the conservative parties to influence their educational policy with such success that a pressure group was founded, the Defence of Government Schools, to counter their efforts.

Not surprisingly, in the midst of this increased activity by pressure groups, the teachers themselves attempted with some success to exert more power upon the outcome of what was essentially a political fight for resources. It was not just that teachers began to develop subject associations in which to pursue purely professional problems. What had traditionally been thought of as a relatively quiet and respectable minor profession came to be seen as a conflictful group very prone to strike. Much of their activity was associated with such industrial matters as salaries and conditions of service, but a number of the aims pursued by industrial means were professional in character (B. Bessant and A.D. Spaull, 1972). Examples were the struggle in Victoria over inspection and external examinations. A well-qualified, truly professional teacher, one who, in Beeby's terminology, was in the stage of Meaning, saw the visit of an inspector to assess him for promotion as an insult. Furthermore the fact that external examinations, set by universities outside the control of the teaching force, appeared to specify much of the secondary curriculum, was also contrary to the new professional ideal since fully competent teachers could develop their own curricula to meet local conditions and individual needs. Such arguments were also reinforced by left wing beliefs that favoured schools run by teachers themselves and that aimed to provide wider opportunities at both secondary and tertiary level to disadvantaged students.

The battle in Victoria led in 1976 to the establishment of the Victorian Institute of Secondary Education which, it is planned, will take over the running of the university entrance examination in addition to many other activities associated with the secondary schools. Upon this statutory body are representatives of many of the pressure groups interested in the decisions made about secondary education, including those that affect the curriculum. Thus the Education Department, the teachers in state and independent schools, the tertiary institutions—no longer only the universities—, industry, commerce and parents are all involved. This body, and those like it in other States, recognise that the control exercised by the universities has deep political implications. It is because of this that the proper position of the so-called profession of teaching in this process is so difficult to define. Teachers have claimed that, as professional experts, they should control the curriculum, but, certainly in Victoria, they have also supported a measure of participation in school government by such lay persons as parents. There is a conflict here: when can the layman tell the expert what to do? In addition, in the final judgement under the democratic system by which Australia is governed, the Government, on behalf of the taxpayer, decides how taxes are to be spent, and teachers may find in specific cases that the decision may go against their professional view of what should happen. In these cases the scope and nature of the political activity to be taken is always in doubt and inevitably conflict over control of the curriculum will occur.

Since the 1960s, the situation has grown more complex because the Commonwealth has increased the financial aid that it gives to education through the States. First, in 1959 the Australian Universities Commission was established and responsibility for the universities was accepted; in 1967 a similar commission was set up to watch over higher technical education, and, finally, in 1972 the teachers colleges were included in this latter arrangement. Since power lies with the purse-strings, tertiary education is now in great measure controlled from Canberra. However the situation below the tertiary level is more complex, particularly as at the primary and secondary levels both state and independent schools exist. In 1973, as a result of an initiative of the first Whitlam Government, the Interim Committee of the Schools Commission reported, recommending methods by which finance could be made available from the Commonwealth (or, as it was now known, the Australian) Government through the States to both state and private schools, largely for schools that could be seen as disadvantaged. The Schools Commission was established in 1973 as a statutory body to recommend on such funding. There were two important implications of these changes. Firstly, the independent schools had to set up bureaucratic channels to process applications and the distribution of such funding; in effect, the Australian Government had triggered off the establishment of a separate formal private educational system. Secondly, the provision of such funds from Canberra was not entirely without strings; it was given on certain conditions and, therefore, carried an element of central control.

The Schools Commission itself was in a position to influence curricular developments in a number of ways. This in its early days a working party was established to examine the place of girls in schools. In its report, published in 1975, to which reference will be made in the next chapter, much was said about the curriculum. In addition to such attempts to change the climate of curricular opinion small grants have been made directly to schools to finance innovations in, amongst other things, the curriculum. Another federal source of finance for such purposes during this period has been the Educational Research and Development Council (ERDC), established in 1971. The ERDC has given grants for developmental work in, for example, the

Social Studies, as well as for research projects that relate to the bases of curricular theory, for example, to investigate the way children's thinking develops in the field of Mathematics and Science.

One other central initiative occurred in 1973 when the Australian Government promised to establish a Curriculum Development Centre (CDC). This statutory body, financed by the central Government, began work in the same year, though the legal processes to establish it were not complete until mid-1975. The CDC has been given a wide remit in the field of curricular development and research; in addition it has to diffuse information about, supply schools with, and may itself publish curricular materials. Again it has a political task in that the States are represented on the Council and are, therefore, in a strong position to try to influence the CDC, though, of course, the CDC may work to form the views of the States so that they support its plans.

In brief, since 1945, after a period of prosperous inertia, the Australian Government has begun to make incursions into the financing of, and hence the control of, education—an area previously entirely the responsibility of the States and still seen by many as mainly in the power of the States. A more egalitarian and individualist ideology is being used, particularly by the new middle class, to justify action in relation to education. Thus the conflicts between pressure groups, and especially those initiated by teachers associations, have become more intense. Furthermore recently signs have appeared that the greater freedom fought for in the decade around 1970 is seen by some to have become too wide, so that the proponents of more conservative ideologies are beginning to reassert themselves.

(iii) Education. In 1936 Britain legislated that the school leaving age would be raised to fifteen from 1939; the war delayed action, however, until 1947. In the same year, 1936, a conference of Australian Directors of Education recommended to the States' Ministers to take the same action from 1940. During the 1940s, each State did legislate to raise the minimum school leaving age, though, except in Tasmania and New South Wales, action waited until the 1960s. The result of this legislation, taken together with the tendency for adolescents to stay longer at school, was a staggering rise in the population of young people staying at secondary school beyong the age at which they might leave. The percentages of various age groups in Australia who were still at school rose as follows between 1958 and 1968: fifteen-year-olds from 40 to 78, sixteen-year-olds from 22 to 48 and seventeen-year-olds from 8 to 25 (R.T. Fitzgerald, 1970: 16–19). For this reason,

as will be seen, during the period since the end of the war the secondary curriculum has become a major focus of interest for educationalists and others.

By the early 1950s a revision of primary curricula was under way in most States. This was seen as necessary for no other reason than that the last major revisions had been made in the 1920s and 1930s. A number of characteristics marked the changes. The intensity of study demanded was lessened. There was an attempt to build on the currently fashionable psychological concept of 'readiness' so that skills in, for example, Reading and Mathematics were matched, it was hoped, to the mental capabilities of individual children. More time was given to subjects outside the main core of the three R's; Art, Manual Work, Music and Physical Education all received more attention. The tendency was to emphasise the total development of the individual child at the expense of the teaching of the various types of competency needed by society. In 1962 the ACER ran an important conference in Melbourne, attended by influential figures from each State. At this meeting these ideas were linked to one other concept that was then becoming increasingly important, namely ungraded classes. The title of the report of this conference, *Each One is Different* (G.W. Bassett, 1964), admirably sums up the central educational ideology of the time in relation to primary schools. Teachers, it was recommended, should very rarely teach classes as a whole, and then only in the new subjects of Art/Craft, Science and Social Studies, and sometimes in Mathematics. For the rest the individual children in classes, ungraded by ability and of a similar age, should proceed through materials that were not prescribed for specific grades at the rate most suited to each one of them. Teachers were, in a word, to individualise instruction.

The demands put upon teachers were different in such a system from those when a formal syllabus, prescribed by grade, was in use. A very different preparation was necessary for the new breed of teachers. Indeed even in Queensland and Victoria, the strongholds of the pupil-teacher method of training, the switch to pre-service preparation had been made before the war. Primary teachers now have a wide secondary education and a tertiary education in some academic subjects, so that they have a strong background from which to provide lesson material across the wide range of subjects with which the class teacher in the primary school must deal. Furthermore they are now trained to cope flexibly in the classroom; there is no longer necessarily one right method which must be used and of which the Department approves. There is evidence, at least in Victoria, that primary teachers feel competent to develop their own curricula in all areas except one, Mathematics[3], a subject in which there has been a growing weakness in secondary schools since the 1950s; this problem has been most serious amongst girls, who have traditionally provided the majority of entrants to primary teaching.

The word often used in relation to secondary schools since the 1950s has been 'crisis'. This serious situation was mainly caused by three closely linked tendencies. There was, firstly, the huge rise in enrolments to which reference has already been made. This was not only caused by the higher minimum school leaving age, but also by the rising birth-rate, the increase in immigration and by the prosperity of the country which allowed, even encouraged, parents to keep their children at school. This rise, secondly, had implications for the nature of the students in secondary schools; they no longer necessarily came from homes where education was highly valued and an increasingly large number of migrants spoke English in a restricted manner. Finally, the very prosperity which made the expansion of schooling possible and desirable also tempted many teachers, especially with tertiary qualifications, out of the teaching force into industry. Between 1955 and 1967 the proportion of the total teaching force who were in secondary schools rose by 15 per cent, but the percentage of those with tertiary qualifications only rose by 3 per cent. The quality of secondary teachers measured in this way varied by State; thus, the variation in 1960 was from 65.8 per cent with university qualifications in Victoria to 25.9 per cent in Queensland. This index of quality is probably too severe in that no account is taken of the increasing population of secondary teachers with a broader secondary schooling and a fuller non-university-level teacher training. Certainly, greater freedom in all sorts of ways was given to these teachers. A bizarre symbol of this was the belated abandoning, in 1966, of the requirement that Victorian teachers, including secondary, should sign a time book; schools were now themselves responsible for ensuring that teachers kept school hours. But the major loosening of control related to curricula, and followed upon the gradual elimination of external examinations except at year twelve, though changes were also made at that level.

---

3. A.M. Rice, Planned Change, Organisational Innovations and Patterns of Implementation with Particular Reference to the Curriculum, Ph. D. thesis, Monash University, 1978.

One major series of changes to examinations occurred in New South Wales where, as a result of the report in 1957 of a committee chaired by H.S. Wyndham, the Director-General of Education, a new system of external examinations was introduced in 1962. External examinations were to be set at years ten and twelve. They were based on a compulsory core and a number of electives; the core included English, Mathematics, Science, Art, Music and Physical Education. Subjects could be taken at three levels; Pass, Credit and Advanced. Many of the tendencies which operated more strongly later in this period can be noted here: the belief that as many students as possible shall be given the chance to achieve something; the support for a broad core, much less utilitarian than formerly; and the opportunity for choice by students.

More recently, in Queensland, all external examinations have been eliminated. There is, however, a system whereby moderated school-based results are available to those who want them, for example, universities, so that entrance standards to tertiary education can be maintained. Over the same period in Victoria a more gradual process, characterised by many similar tendencies, has occurred. In 1967, the Intermediate (year ten) and in 1972 the Leaving (year eleven) examinations were eliminated. The Higher School Certificate (HSC) itself has undergone significant changes so that elective sections have been admitted, a degree of school-based marking is now allowed in some subjects, and, finally, the range of subjects has been extended to include Domestic Science, Environmental Science, several migrant and Asian languages and Legal Studies. Clearly, the result of all these moves has been to lessen the external constraints, especially of the universities, on the curriculum, particularly in the lower forms, since the effect of prescription at year twelve on some subjects is minimal for lower years. It should be noted that this liberalising effect is least noticeable in the modern utilitarian Australian version of the traditional secondary curriculum consisting, as it does, of Mathematics and Science.

The aim and ethos of the high school changed greatly during the post-war years. At the beginning of the period the state-provided secondary schools were still élitist in spirit and curriculum, imitative of and competitive with the independent schools. As the proportion of those staying on rose there was a shift in aim; the belief had been that there should be access for all students to those parts of the traditional curriculum with which they could cope. However the growing realisation that the new secondary students were very different in nature from those of the late 1960s forced a reconsideration of the curriculum for mass secondary education. The high school came to be seen as the common school for all children in its catchment area. This change occurred at a time when there was much argument, based on British experience, about streaming. Conditions here were now very different from Britain since the high school could not be compared with either the élite grammar school or the lower status modern school. Yet it could be seen as very like the new comprehensive school. The aim, therefore, expressed in its most ideal form, became that there should be access for all students to all knowledge. Eventually, as the more radical ideas of the late sixties became more influential, this ideal was changed to a demand that all students have access to the knowledge that they wished. This was a more individual version of the ideal, in that it allowed for choice and denied prescription in curricula.

The logical consequences of mass secondary education were many, but one problem was central. There had always been children who for one reason or another failed to complete satisfactorily what was seen as the course of the primary school. Now these children, regardless of their educational competence, were legally bound to undergo a secondary course. Clearly the traditional curriculum, aimed at the university or entry to some middle class occupation was not likely to be suitable for a group of students whose intellectual capacities and interests were very diverse.

One State, in particular, Victoria, grappled early with these problems. In 1966, the year in which the Intermediate examination was abolished, the Director of Secondary Education, R.A. Reed, founded a new body called the Curriculum Advisory Board, consisting mainly of teachers, but also containing representation from the universities and other interested groups. In 1967 he circulated four papers to schools, asking that staff meet and send comments, via regional meetings, back to him. The answers were then, in 1968, discussed at a seminar on the secondary curriculum at Burwood Teachers College. As a result a number of broad, but radical principles were agreed upon as the basis upon which curricula were to be reconsidered. These saw secondary education as a stage of schooling in its own right and, therefore, not liable to constraints from tertiary bodies. Individuality was to be developed, choice given and processes rather than content were to be the focus in teaching. For a few schools major change followed, more particularly in the adoption of an elective curriculum and in the movement towards much 'integration' of formerly separate subjects. For most schools there was a little change, particularly to teaching some version of what came to be known as Modern Studies, especially in the lower age ranges. This subject was intended to be an integrated version of English, History, Geography, Politics and sometimes even Science, in each case seen in its widest sense and related to the modern world, so that courses about the mass media, law and order, or the environment became common. The eventual effect of Reed's initiative was probably less than was anticipated for two main reasons. Additional funds were needed, for example, to purchase new materials; these were still relatively scarce in the years around 1970. Also great demands for changes in attitudes were put upon teachers and parents; except perhaps for the radical minority, teachers were unprepared to go the whole way with the new principles, and certainly parents continued to see secondary schooling as a utilitarian preparation for a future career—whether for a girl as a wife and mother or for a boy as, say, an apprentice or a professional worker.

Similar tendencies were at work throughout Australia and affected the whole secondary age range in both state and private schools. One measure of many of these new views is the changing popularity of various subjects at the sixth form in internal examinations. Table 4.2 gives the entries for the Victorian HSC in a number of subjects for boys and for girls as a percentage of enrolments at year ten two years earlier. The rise in the popularity of the social sciences (Economics, Social Studies) amongst both boys and girls is clearly visible. The comparative drop in numbers opting for the natural sciences (Physics) is seen, but so, too, is the remarkable growth in the demand for life sciences (Biology), especially amongst girls. The weak position of European modern languages (French) is seen, though during the same period Indonesian and Japanese were introduced and taught to a slowly rising number of students. Finally, a remarkable example of the differences between the courses chosen by girls and by boys is shown in the figures for English Literature. Some further comment will be made in the next chapter of differences by sex in the secondary curriculum. Here attention will now be given to a number of the individual subjects taught in the secondary school.

In English there were great changes from the subject as traditionally taught. The emphasis, on the one hand, had been on grammar, spelling and correct use of language and, on the other, on the close reading of literature seen as worth while, either morally or stylistically. Research, carried out in the 1960s, on children's language showed that the new secondary student had a very different linguistic apparatus

TABLE 4.2: *HSC Entries As a Percentage of Enrolments in Fourth Form*

	1956		1964		1972	
	Boys	**Girls**	**Boys**	**Girls**	**Boys**	**Girls**
Accounting	1.7	0.2	2.8	0.6	8.4	2.8
Biology	3.4	5.8	4.0	8.0	9.0	20.8
Economics	5.6	1.1	11.9	3.6	19.9	10.5
French	5.7	8.9	4.4	11.1	1.4	7.5
Geography	9.5	6.1	12.9	13.5	13.3	16.6
Literature (English)	10.8	13.4	7.3	16.3	8.0	21.4
Physics	19.8	3.6	19.4	5.2	17.3	5.5
Social Studies	4.2	0.5	6.1	2.1	12.4	8.8

Source: R.T. White, VUSEB Circular to Schools, September 1973.

from the traditional student. In view of this and also of his different attitude to school, curricular material that seemed more directly relevant to his life than perhaps Chaucer or Milton came to be used. There was a growing emphasis on reality outside the school, and especially on applying the methods of literary criticism to the products of the various mass media. Instead of *Wuthering Heights* or *Richard Mahony* students studied *Coronation Street* or *Bellbird*. The second major change in direction, and this was as noticeable at the primary as the secondary level, was that children were encouraged to express their own individuality in their writing rather than copy the style of others. Creativity was encouraged, even at the expense of correct grammar or spelling. Much criticism of this tendency has come from employers and those in tertiary education who complain that contemporary school-leavers have a lower standard of written English than previously. It is only recently that in Australia evidence has been gathered that can be used to monitor the schools in such respects and there is little evidence to sustain these accusations. But certainly the demands to maintain traditionally accepted standards of English Expression are a check on the ways in which the tendencies to encourage individuality might work, though it is also worth noting that David Holbrook, a recent visitor from England, who is influential in the field of teaching English, particularly to the less able, felt that Australia had not moved far at all in this new direction.

Amongst the languages other than English that are now taught in schools two changes are worth noting. Firstly, the methods used are now much more realistic in that, since more emphasis is now put upon the ability to speak foreign languages, methods of teaching are encouraged that promote fluency and correct accent rather than the ability to read critically foreign literature. Language laboratories and the use of tapes of native speakers are more common. In some cases there are recent migrants available to assist in the teaching of European languages. But, secondly, there has been a decreasing number of students learning these languages, and particularly the classical languages of Latin and Greek. Indeed, it is now possible to do courses in Classical Civilisation, both in universities and secondary schools, which demand no knowledge of these languages. Within the European languages there has been some growth in the popularity of Italian and Modern Greek at the expense of French and German. But the major change has been the growth in such Eastern languages as Indonesian, Japanese and Chinese, a result of the Australian realisation that she is no longer an extension of the European mother country, but has grown to be a nation in her own right with close relationships with many Asian countries.

In Mathematics there has been a great influence from overseas of curricular development work, in both the United States of America and Britain, in which the emphasis is put upon principles and processes rather than upon computational skills. In the early 1960s the introduction of Cuisenaire rods into the primary school began this process. Perhaps the most recent example of its influence at the secondary level is the introduction of a computer option into the HSC in Victoria and the fairly general acceptance throughout Australia of students' using handheld calculators in schools and in examinations. As in the case of English, the result has been criticism from the public that the young can no longer do simple, quick calculations—in general parlance, 'they don't know their tables'. This is another area where monitoring of what is happening in the schools has begun.

Very similar tendencies have been at work in Science. Rote learning of Boyle's Law may help a student to pass an examination so that he 'gets a better job', but to discover the processes involved himself, even though he cannot express them in scientific jargon, will, it is believed, educate him the more fully. Furthermore the new secondary student cannot, or will not, understand much technical language. Thus problem-centred courses that will seem relevant and that relate to the world outside the school are being taught. The recent rise in interest in courses concerning environmental problems forms one example. Courses of this nature also often aim to 'integrate' the traditional sciences. In Victoria there is now a subject of this nature in the HSC—Environmental Science. All such new ways of teaching demand evaluation so that teachers may know whether or not their aims are being met. In Science much research has been done based on the original work of Bloom and his associates who, in 1956, published a rigorous taxonomy of educational objectives. The new subject of Science Education, now found institutionalised in tertiary institutions in Australia and with its own professional association, has been largely built around the testing of newly developed science curricula, especially those associated with the modern techniques of discovery learning.

The same forces that have been noted as operating in the traditional secondary subjects were even more strongly at work on the new subjects, and especially on Social Studies. This subject was seen as particularly apt for the new secondary student, originally perhaps because it had lower status than the traditional subjects, but eventually because of its relevance to the world beyond the school. It was also seen by those holding more radical ideologies about secondary school organisation as a suitable subject, especially in its newer and more sociological form, both for them to teach and for students to learn, since it seemed to bring into question the authority of tradition. Originally Social Studies had been seen as an integration of the traditional subjects of History, Geography and Civics, but now it came to include, and even at times to be dominated by, Sociology, a subject growing very fashionable at the tertiary level during the troubled years around 1970. In Social Studies relevance to the real world could be very clear. Furthermore, visits, or work, outside the school, often in the form of surveys, were apt and common. In this subject relevance, choice, integration and flexible timetable, the shibboleths of the modern secondary curriculum, seemed to come together in one subject. Very few remembered that much had been done to the same ends in the traditional subject of the Classics, though of course to motivate the new secondary student to learn classical Greek would probably be impossible. By the late 1960s in Australia as a whole, about 70 per cent of pupils at year nine spent an eighth or more of their time on Social Studies. There were great differences, however, between States; in Victoria, which has tended to be a forerunner in this subject, two-thirds of the pupils spent eight or nine periods per week on it, whereas in New South Wales and Queensland the majority gave only four periods per week to Social Studies (D.M. Bennett, 1968).

It would be wrong to say that the independent secondary schools were not influenced by these changes. Certainly in the traditional subjects of Science and Mathematics some of the innovatory curricula were either developed or much used in these schools. So, too, were subjects such as Social Studies introduced, but in these new elements, as in the traditional elements of the curriculum, the emphasis was upon the old virtues of high academic standards and the new methods involved were seen not as necessarily good in themselves in that, for example, they created a different type of personality, but as more efficient methods for teachers to use or for students to learn by or, most of all, for attracting the interest of adolescents.

In one area, because of the nature of their foundations, the independent schools, at both primary and secondary levels, did have a particular interest; this was Religious Education. However this subject was also taught in the secular state schools and here there were pressures for change apart from those already mentioned. Thus the sheer increase in numbers, especially in secondary schools, meant that at a time when fewer religious were being recruited to the various denominations there was a shortage of teachers—there was a drop in Victoria between 1965 and 1973 of those receiving the Council of Christian Education in Schools agreed syllabus from 76.8 to 22.6 per cent of secondary students. Furthermore a growing number of the visiting teachers felt themselves to be ill-equipped to teach the subject —especially when making only one visit per week to a school. Finally, the present organisation of the subject as an option did not encourage students' interest (A.W. Black, 1975). These problems have not yet been solved, particularly because of the lack of acceptance of the recommendations of the various state bodies that have recently reported on Religious Education in Schools.

The Roman Catholic schools have had an additional change. Prior to the 1970s Religious Education had been based on learning and understanding the catechism. 'But although the aim of teaching religion was to draw children to God, the religion lessons consisted of the inculcation of religious faiths through memorisation, a practice condemned by the [Catholic Education] Office in other subject areas.' In secondary schools, in addition, especially after the early 1950s, much attention was given to apologetics, often taught as a very negative set of answers to critics of the Roman Catholic faith, and also to 'the inculcation of social doctrine which emphasised anti-Communism rather than the Church's teachings on social justice'. Great changes of attitude occurred even before Vatican II, but this series of meetings speeded up the introduction of new approaches in the schools. Findings of research by educational psychologists buttressed the new approaches which began "with the experience of the child, rather than with the concepts or a body of truths'. Religious knowledge was now taught to call forth 'a personal faith response to the God-event from the pupil . . . Hence, knowledge requires commitment and action rather than individual assent'.[4] Relevance and individual response were forces also working in the field of Religous Education, and not only amongst Roman Catholics.

Although English, Mathematics and Science, and in the independent schools Religious Education, were still the core of the secondary curriculum, an increasing amount of time was coming to be given to Music, Art and Craft, Social Studies and, even for boys now, to Domestic Science. Furthermore it was no longer the less gifted who had to do these subjects; they were now justified no longer on the grounds of vocational, but of aesthetic development which was needed by all—perhaps especially by the academically gifted. A far wider choice of art or craft forms was now available in schools; there were, for example, printing, sculpture, pottery, weaving and jewellery. Indeed, this subject was coming to be known as 'Artcraft', and under international influences 'creativity and self-expression became established as dominant universal objectives for both art and craft activities in schools'.[5]

Secondary schools were now also being asked to undertake the teaching of a number of subjects that were previously taken for granted as being the responsibility of the family. Such were Sex Education, Driver Education and Consumer Education. By the end of the 1970s the focus of the argument about what secondary schools should teach out of the welter of requests made to them seemed to be settling down on attempts to justify a core, together with a number of options from which students could choose. The aim very definitely for most schools had become that their students should enter adulthood as competent citizens rather than as competent to proceed to the tertiary level of education.

Nowhere were the problems concerning the secondary curriculum seen more clearly than in the arguments about alternative forms of schooling. Originally the progressive school movement had been peculiar to the private sector, but during the late 1960s, and in Victoria after Reed's initiatives, alternative schools were financed out of taxes within the state-provided system. Three important tendencies should

---

4. H.M. Praetz, Ideology, Authority and Power in the Catholic Education System, unpublished Ph.D. thesis, Monash University, 1978.
5. G. Hammond, *op.cit.*

be mentioned. Some schools were built, especially in South Australia and the Australian Capital Territory, on an open plan, so that the relationships between teachers and taught, between students, and between subjects became changed; the hope is that authority will be challenged, both in relation to personal hierarchy and to the received knowledge associated with the traditional curriculum. Secondly, community schools have been established, several of which are in Victoria; the main aims are twofold: to break down the boundaries between school and the outside world so that learning is a more real experience, and also so that non-members of the school may participate in schools, the aim being that the curriculum will gain a dimension of reality. Lastly, several learning exchanges have been set up, following the proposals of the radical author, Ivan Illich; here the intention is to match anyone who has a particular resource which he wishes to add to the available stock in the schools to someone who has expressed a wish to learn from that particular resource—the apotheosis of a curriculum based upon choice from electives, as the whole community should become available as curricular material (R.T. Fitzgerald, J.K. Matthews, P.P. Thomson, 1973).

To summarise the changes to the curricula at both primary and secondary levels since 1945 is a daunting task, partly because we are still so close to the period, but partly because these changes have not yet worked themselves out entirely. However clearly the movement has been in the direction of what Beeby called the stage of Meaning. 'Process' not 'product' and discovery not rote learning have come to matter, although, even with a teaching force of high quality, curricula based on such principles are difficult to develop for and teach to the new secondary student. The age of mass secondary education may be nearer in Australia, but the wider opportunities being offered in this new era have not yet been matched by an equally wide range of curricula and pedagogies.

3. Conclusion

W.F. Connell (1970) has spoken of the three myths of Australian education. These he believes to be individual opportunity, education for citizenship, and thoroughness. Each seems truly to be a myth. Only recently, and not generally, have individuals come anywhere near being able to have the opportunity to undertake a curriculum that would develop their own potentialities or, though we are not so concerned with this point here, to have the chance to spend as long in education as they wish. The aimed-for distribution of the stock of knowledge in many ways remains a restricted one. Education for citizenship begs the question: for what sort of society? Certainly until 1945 most children were taught to sit still, to be loyal to the mother country, and political criticism was discouraged. Any attempt today to teach about the currently critical problems of our society, for example, about China or the family or about the mining of uranium, can meet much opposition. Those in power do not wish the present distribution of knowledge to be changed or even challenged. Finally, thoroughness formerly meant rote learning, not a thorough understanding; now, rote learning having to a great extent disappeared from our schools, the cries have re-emerged for rote learning—for a move back from the stage of Meaning to that of Formalism. Radical changes in the distribution of knowledge rarely go unchallenged.

The question of the purpose of Meaning, once the schools have reached that stage, is being posed elsewhere than in Australia. Australian education, whether in relation to curriculum, pedagogy or structure, has always been derivative and eclectic, originally owing to the difficulty of disentangling itself from its colonial apron-strings, but more recently because of the great ease of international communication. But in addition there has been a tendency to convert theories from overseas into slogans so that in a not oversubtle way vital application of any theory fails. Thus the project method became a pedagogical trick, not a radical reform. Two reasons for this tendency may be advanced; firstly, there is the tight control that state departments have kept over the schools until very recent years, but, secondly, there is the fact that there have been no local intellectual prophets. Ideas are imported and, when applied at second or third hand, lose their cutting edge.

In this way the Australian element in curricula is determined by local social conditions. For example, despite the beginning of a movement towards regionalisation in the state educational systems, the tendency to centralisation in administration is still a very strong influence. The great severity of the depression of the 1930s made resources scarce so that the version of progressive education of the time was very much diluted in its application in Australia. Differences in the political arrangments for local government here mean that the ideological demand for participation in schools is worked out in a different way from, say, in Britain. The Australian demographic structure forced a bigger crisis in secondary education when the clamour for mass secondary schooling came than was the case in many other societies. In each of these examples the peculiarities of Australian social structure have resulted in a different response to changing ideological climates from that found when similar forces were at work overseas.

Finally, though Australia has achieved mass primary education and is some way along the road to mass secondary education, R.F. Butts would, in 1978, in all likelihood still make the same comment about schooling that he made in 1955,

> I find very strong the assumption that a little education is good for all children, but much education is good only for a few.
>
> (R.F. Butts, 1955: 37)

There has been a movement, as Beeby predicted, from dame schools through Formalism to a curriculum dedicated to the understanding of Meaning, but the chance to study this curriculum is not as widely available as it might be, and, perhaps more important, many of those with power over the education system would seem to be afraid of the results for them if the masses came to understand more meaningfully.

Bibliography

BUTTS, R.F. (1955): *Assumptions Underlying Australian Education*. A.C.E.R.: Melbourne. An overseas visitor's view of Australian schools in the mid-1950s.

CLEVERLEY, J. and LAWRY, J. (1972): *Australian Education in the Twentieth Century*. Longmans: Camberwell (Vic.). A collection of papers which are essential reading for anyone interested in the recent history of Australian education.

CONNELL, W.F. (1970): 'Myths and Traditions in Australian Education', *Australian Journal of Education* 14 (3). An account based in social history of the *ideés recues* of Australian education.

FITZGERALD, R.T. (1970): *The Secondary School at Sixes and Sevens*. A.C.E.R.: Hawthorn (Vic.). A detailed account of qualitative and quantitiative trends in secondary schooling around 1970.

HUNT, F.J. (1972): 'Society, Schooling and the Individual', *Australian Journal of Education* 16 (1). An analysis of some of the main ideological forces at work in the early 1970s, especially in relation to compulsory education.

MANDELSON, L.A. (1974): Australian Primary Education, 1919–1939: A Study of Inertia, Continuity and Change in State-Controlled Schooling, unpublished Ph.D. thesis, University of Sydney. A major, if not the only, detailed source for this topic in the interwar years.

Other References

AUSTIN, A.G. and SELLECK, R.J.W. (1975): *The Australian Government School 1830–1914*, Pitman: Carlton (Vic.).

BASSETT, G.W. (1964): *Each One is Different*. A.C.E.R.: Melbourne.

BENNETT, D.M. (1968): 'The Study of Society in Australian Secondary Schools', *Quarterly Review of Australian Education* 2 (1).

BESSANT, B. and SPAULL, A.D. (1972): *Teachers in Conflict*. Melbourne University Press: Melbourne.

BLACK, A.W. (1975): 'Religious Studies in Australian Schools', *Australian Education Review* 7 (3).

CRANE, A.R. and WALKER, W.G. (1957): *Peter Board: His Contribution to the Development of Education in New South Wales*. A.C.E.R.: Melbourne.

CUNNINGHAM, K.S. (1972). 'Ideas, Theories and Assumptions in Australian Education', in Cleverley, J. and Lawry, J., eds, *Australian Education in the Twentieth Century*. Longmans: Camberwell (Vic.).

FITZGERALD, R.T., MATTHEWS, J.K. and THOMPSON, P.P. (1973): 'Alternative Education', *Quarterly Review of Australian Education* 6 (3).

LAWRY, J. (1972): 'Understanding Australian Education 1901–1914', in Cleverley, J. and Lawry, J. eds, *op.cit.*

5. The Changing Australian Moral Curriculum

We are so accustomed to believing that emulation is the essential motivating force in academic life, that we cannot easily imagine how a school could exist which did not have a carefully worked out system of graduated rewards in order to keep the enthusiasm of the pupils perpetually alive. Good marks, solemn statements of satisfactory performance, distinctions, competitive essays, prize-givings: all these seem to us, in differing degrees, the necessary accompaniments to any social education system.

(E. Durkheim, 1977: 159)

In the last two chapters the emphasis has been almost completely upon the academic curriculum. The analysis has been concerned with what selection of academic knowledge it was planned to transmit to the next generation and whether or not that selection in some sense matched what various groups with power in society considered was needed. Except inasmuch as this knowledge might be used to keep the society running smoothly, we have not given any attention either to how knowledge might in general be used or, more fundamentally, how future adults might be taught to behave towards one another. It is true that Australian schools seem to have concentrated upon useful learning, that is upon the vocational aspect of any possible curriculum, but they have not done so to the total exclusion of teaching morality. Even though students may not have realised it and even though teachers may have sometimes disclaimed it, the Australian school, especially the independent one, did give some priority to the moral curriculum.

Morality may be taught either directly or indirectly. Direct teaching may, for example, be concerned with what behaviour is deemed to be good or bad. Indirect teaching may occur in three main ways. Firstly, the school may be organised in such a way that certain behaviour is inevitably encouraged or discouraged, though no overt teaching takes place; thus the compulsory wearing of school uniform usually has some constraining effects on behaviour. Next the direct teaching of some academic subjects, for example Religious Education or History, may have an indirect moral effect. Lastly, such so-called extra-curricular activities as team games have, particularly in the independent secondary schools, been given a major part in teaching certain personality traits, as, for example, co-operation.

In this chapter each of these three methods of indirect teaching will be considered in turn since there seems to be in Australian schools remarkably little direct teaching of Moral Education unlike in contemporary Britain, where this subject is now found on the time-tables of some schools. In whatever way it is undertaken, the inculcation of the contemporary code of morality to its young is a process vital to the rulers of any society since they wish to ensure that moral behaviour matches the social norms that they support. Deviance is not wanted, more especially because it can so easily initiate opposition or change. In examining the Australian moral curriculum, the same social setting and the same situation in relation to the control of the educational system as in the last two chapters will be assumed, except where specific comment to the contrary is made.

1. Organisation

i) *The Independent Schools.* At the start of the nineteenth century the English independent schools were in many respects at a low ebb; especially low were their moral standards. Some attempts at reform had begun when in 1828 Thomas Arnold was appointed headmaster of Rugby School. Although he died comparatively soon in 1842, Arnold had by then made major changes at Rugby, using ideas both of his own and borrowed from others, so that his school became widely known and was taken as a model throughout the country.

Arnold was particularly interested in raising the moral tone of his school which, like most similar schools, was characterised by cribbing in academic work, by bullying and by general moral laxity. He had much success in ridding Rugby of most of these vices by establishing an organisational system based on close supervision of the sixth form by himself, by giving power to sixth formers, especially to prefects, over the general administration of the rest of the school, and by ensuring that housemasters thoroughly supervised the pupils in their care. In addition, he made the chapel a central focus of the school and extended the school's moral empire by controlling spare time as well as lesson time through the new emphasis he put on team games.

In the 1820s to 1830s, when the first few independent schools were established in Australia, they were set up on the English model because their masters inevitably based them upon what they themselves knew. But when the colonies expanded after 1850 and the increased demand for secondary education in Australia led to the growth of a greater supply of such schools, the Arnoldian revolution had taken place. Thus, for example, in Victoria, Scotch College (1851), Geelong Grammar School (1857) and Melbourne Grammar School (1858), and in South Australia St Peter's (1847), were all founded at the time when the new ideas were very much in the air. Turney (1967) has shown how several such schools in New South Wales had as leaders men who had been inspired by Arnold when pupils or masters under him in England.

The schools founded at this time did not all prosper, but most of the well-known contemporary independent schools have their origins in the 1850s to 1860s and were deeply influenced by Arnold's ideas. They built a strong tradition and have become examplars of a certain type of education of the whole man (I.V. Hansen, 1971). They, therefore, give a high priority to the moral side of the curriculum. They tend to have firm goals of a moral nature. Because most of these schools were founded by religious bodies and because morality has so close a connection with religion the goals tend to be seen in Christian terms. Arnold is said to have aimed to produce 'Christian gentlemen'. However the important point to note here is that when educational goals are closely specified, it becomes possible to create an organisation geared to achieving these goals and, furthermore, it becomes easy to evaluate whether or not a school is meeting its goals. Schools with clearly defined goals have been shown empirically to yield the desired results more often than those where they are loosely specified (H.T. Himmelweit and B. Swift, 1969). In broad terms, educational goals are often categorised as being traditional or progressive in nature.

a) **Traditional.** Particularly in traditional education, aims are often hidden in the ritual elements of school organisation. Basically, traditional education is concerned with discipline, hard work and hierarchy. The English schools that were originally influenced by Arnold were all boarding schools and, therefore, could exert near total control over the waking hours of their pupils. In this context, they had a high chance of successfully inculcating their moral curriculum in any child, especially, as was usual, if he came from a home in which the same standards were supported.

Yet the independent schools developed in Australia in a way somewhat different from in the mother country. The main difference was that in most Australian independent schools there came to be more day-boys, or day-girls, than boarders. However the main organisational features of the English public school reappeared in Australia, and with largely the same moral aims. The schools were single-sex schools. The question of the separate schooling of boys and girls will be taken up below, but certainly this rigid division of the sexes at school did parallel the segregated sex roles of Australian society. Hence these schools came to emphasise so-called male and female qualities in the respective sexes and, in addition, to transmit what were seen as the right ways of behaving towards the other sex.

The independent schools were, as indicated, Christian and all denominations established schools in the Arnoldian mould. They, therefore, had a chapel, taught Religious Education, and respected a pastoral tradition. There grew up an articulated system of chaplain, housemaster and/or tutor to watch over the development of each pupil, whether boarder or day boy. If anecdote means anything, such systems were stronger in Roman Catholic than in Protestant schools. A pastoral system implies a hierarchy and the hierarchies of independent secondary schools were highly developed. The headmaster at the top devolved responsibilities to his housemasters, they to tutors and to prefects who, in turn, might hold their powers in relation to the school as a whole or to house activities alone. Pupils wore uniforms, but their positions in the hierarchy were often marked by small differences either in the uniform itself or in the way it was worn—for example, the prefects might wear a different tie and also they might be allowed to wear their jackets unbuttoned.

Anyone who has watched the students of an independent secondary school gathering for morning assembly, often in the school chapel, will have seen the lessons of the moral curriculum being taught through ritual. Hierarchy is emphasised in the seating position and in the order of filing into assembly so that deference to authority is emphasised. The authority of religion is automatically stressed, but school announcements concerning disciplinary matters and even sporting results are coupled with religion because they are made by the Head, still sometimes a clergyman, in this assembly.

There is an élite in all such schools, to which pupils are encouraged to aspire, though, to use the phrase that comes naturally in this context, many are called, but few are chosen. Arnold's aim, at least in part, had been to prepare his senior boys for leadership and for service to others in after life by holding responsibility for others at school. His Christian gentlemen were to enter the professions or become politicians or, as colonial administrators, to bear the white man's burden. They were, in other words, very often to give more in time and energy than was measured by the monetary rewards that they received. Such qualities were not perhaps so well suited for the role of entrepreneur in the nineteenth century economy or for life in the loosely structured society of the Australian colonies during the latter part of the nineteenth century, though, it must be admitted, there was competition within the schools to reach the top. Certainly, these schools are structured today to encourage such striving. As one boy at an independent school put it in the mid-1960s:

> . . . there's a clear pecking order . . . I think prefects begin in Form
> III. There are certain obvious moves you must make in order to
> be recognised. First you get on the Library staff . . .
>
> (I.V. Hansen, 1971: 104)

In other words, the environment is, as Durkheim noted in the quotation at the head of this chapter, a competitive one. So that all kinds of ways of being noticed exist—results in class or in examinations, success on the games field or in other forms of extracurricular activity. So it is that many assembly halls, and even chapels, have honours boards hanging in them as ritual incentives to the present pupils to strive for success as their forebears did. Prizes are given for successes in work or at play and in recent years they have been awarded for moral excellence—material haloes for apparently perfect pupils.

It is worth noting that the organisation as described so far is now perhaps rarely found in quite this form. Prize days still exist, but many more receive prizes than did in the past—special arrangements are made so that any one pupil cannot win more than, say, three prizes. Prefects still exist, but now often are elected and see themselves to be responsible for younger students rather than in authority over them. The hierarchy is perceived as shorter, even between staff and students, and authority is no longer absolute, but is subject to criticism and to an element of democratic control. But the lessons of deference, of service, of responsible working for others, and of co-operation in a society of human beings are still taught, albeit in a somewhat less extreme form.

The independent schools tend to be seen as secondary in their age range. They very often have primary, usually known as preparatory, schools associated with them. Little is known, even in Britain, about the detailed history, operation or functions of these schools, but certainly there, as in Australia, they have in the main developed in the image of the secondary schools for which they are preparing.

Finally, there is a tendency to see the independent schools as very conservative. Though they have some deeply held and unchanging goals, especially in relation to the presentation of high moral and academic standards, we must beware of thinking that they will not use modern methods to achieve their ends. Thus Melbourne Grammar School has been a pioneer in converting its library into a resources centre and Geelong Grammar—amongst others—in establishing an adventure school in the bush, but these seeming great changes are made in the service of traditional academic and moral aims, respectively, to teach boys to use all types of materials in the service of good learning and to have the initiative, self-reliance, and physical and moral toughness to cope with difficult individual or group situations. Aims are traditional and perennial, but the pedagogies used to achieve them may change and be modern in style if need be, though not, of course, merely for the sake of being up to date.

b) Progressive. When considering the academic curriculum, we noted that progressive schools came to be founded in the interwar years as a small but slowly growing proportion of the middle class began to feel that the independent schools of the traditional type did not fit their needs. The progressive schools rested much of their existence not so much upon their claim to teach a different curriculum, though there were different emphases, as upon their hope that they would produce a different type of personality in their students. It was, therefore, their moral curriculum that was important. What were their aims in this respect and how did they organise themselves to achieve them?

In comparison with the traditional schools those running progressive schools put a greater emphasis upon the individual child and his development as an individual. They paid less attention to the demands of society in educating a child—the words 'pupil' or 'student' were rarely, if ever, used in these schools. Because the individual pattern of growth was so important, each child has to be allowed as much free choice as possible concerning what he should do. Thus elective systems were important. Furthermore since individual differences were to be encouraged, tolerance of individuality was essential. Clearly in an atmosphere of choice and tolerance, the idea of hierarchy did not fit well so that the difference between teacher and taught was reduced to a minimum. As a result deference no longer became so important a characteristic. Moreover since all the individuals in the school were equally important, all should take part in running it. Hence such schools as Koornung made the participation of the children in their organisation an important part of the curriculum.

The aim was an active, questing, creative child, though this was also said by traditional schools to be, at least in part, their aim. But the progressive schools were organised to allow more emphasis to be put on freedom. The problem for parents was that, though they wanted a different type of personality in their child than they believed the traditional moral curriculum could provide, they also wanted him to maintain the middle class position into which he had been born. Hence they believed that a 'good' secondary education, that is, one academic in emphasis, was necessary, since this would ensure success in life. Progressive schools are, therefore, strongest at the primary level. Their methods did, however, have some small influence on some independent secondary schools. In Chapter 1 we cited the curriculum of Melbourne Girls Grammar School in the period just after World War II. This school was organised around the ideals of choice and of pupil participation in an attempt to gain the benefits of progressive methods in a large single-sex and fairly traditional secondary school. These methods had, however, little or no influence in the state schools, despite Peter Board's experiment at Brighton-le-Sands in the 1920s. Such schools, it was said, could not permit experiment. The average citizen would not see progressivism as really important until it was put into practice in the state schools and, as we shall see below, this has only happened in the very recent past in Australian state schools.

ii)   State Schools. The schools provided by the State have to cater for a wide range of clients, many of whom have views not held by the majority, particularly in relation to the moral curriculum. Thus the children of Roman Catholics, who have always formed a very substantial proportion of the Australian population, sit down in school with the children of other sects or of agnostics. What shall be said of divorce or abortion? The children of socialists and of conservatives attend the same lessons in Social Studies. What shall be taught about democracy? Furthermore parents have usually considered themselves to be ignorant about the academic curriculum, which is in the hands, as they see it, of the experts, the teachers, but they have always had strong views about the moral curriculum, about what is right and what is wrong; they have been willing to state their views, and sometimes have worked to achieve what they see as right even when the schools have tried to do something different.

Two examples of this process may be cited. The first relates to the place of the flag-raising ceremony which, certainly since World War I, has been a focus for disagreement. The aim of this ceremony was to teach patriotism and loyalty to Australia and, because of the nature of the flag, to the British Empire (later, Commonwealth). Yet during World War I, when conscription was such a hard-fought issue, this ceremony was inevitably seen by many as political manipulation and jingoistic. Furthermore in a nation in which there were so many of Irish blood, the idea of loyalty to a British Australia or a British Empire was unlikely to escape criticism. The existence in the interwar years of the League of Nations was another complicating issue, because many supporters of the Labor Party saw the flag-raising ceremony as an attack on the concept of the brotherhood of nations. For such reasons, this ceremony, a part of the moral curriculum, was the centre for much argument.

A recent series of case studies of five Victorian high schools (R.T. Fitzgerald, P.W. Musgrave, D.W. Pettit, 1976) has shown that in such schools parents do see teachers as academic experts, but see themselves as competent to comment upon the moral curriculum. In one of the schools studied, a rural school, a local political group brought much pressure to bear upon the school to withdraw from use in English lessons such works as J.D. Salinger: *Catcher in the Rye* and Barry Oakley: *A Salute to the Great McCarthy*. Though they were unsuccessful in this, they did have one textbook, used in lessons on marriage and the family in Social Studies, withdrawn. This group achieved a situation where the principal and staff were constantly on a careful watch over the moral implications of their teaching.

Until the 1850s, the elementary school in Australia, as in the mother country, was in the main provided by the various religious demoninations. There was, therefore, a very strong influence upon these schools from the Christian ethic of the time. The charity school for the nineteenth century working class does not now seem to us to have been marked by a strong sense of personal charity. Unquestioning obedience to authority was expected at the risk of severe punishment. To some extent the numbers in most classes, up to seventy in urban areas, made little else possible. The textbooks of the time were written to compel acceptance of such moral lessons. Reading books contained moral precepts and stories with very clear moral lessons.

After the 1850s, the effects of the Gold Rushes upon the ethos of the colonies made some version of such a morality seem even more necessary to those in power. Instability, unpredictability and insecurity appeared to have become common. Social anarchy was believed to be close at hand. Hard work no longer provided the only or the most obvious route to material success. Australia seemed to be on the way to becoming a land of larrikins. As in Chartist England, the schoolmaster was seen to be the easiest replacement for the policeman or the soldier, never popular agents of respectability in an Australia with close memories of convict times. So the rote-learning methods associated with the system of payment by results seemed most apt in their encouragement of deference, obedience and the one right answer. Order and tidiness were also easily associated with such a system. Reliance upon such a moral curriculum was further supported because of the nature of those who, at the time, were the main proponents of education—the 'respectable' groups. These were, in the main, doctors, lawyers, clergymen, journalists, merchants and small businessmen, and civil servants. It was from such groups, too, that the parliamentarians were increasingly drawn who, when members of the party in government, had control over the state-provided educational system.

One of the key concepts in the moral curriculum of the elementary school at the time was that of 'good habits'. The word 'good' begged the question of whose values were to define what was to be allowed as worth while. We have seen that the values were those of the then 'respectable' groups. But the traits of personality taught were to become habitual, unquestioned, taken for granted. We are here concerned with moral recipe knowledge and with a situation where its questioning, at least by those who went to or had been at elementary schools, was not to be allowed. There is a paradox here which social historians have as yet not fully explained. There is no doubt that the elementary school at the turn of the century did teach such a moral curriculum. There is also no doubt that the Australian troops in World War I demonstrated a very different form of discipline, much freer in essence, from that of British troops or from the type that would have been predicted in view of the elementary schooling undergone by these soldiers as boys. Assuming that the schools were successful in their efforts, and this assumption can also be questioned, the solution to the problem may lie in the egalitarian nature of adult life, at least in myth, which may temper the 'good' habit of ready deference when once school is ended.

There has been a slow, steady movement to free the primary schools from the old deadening spirit of the elementary system, an attempt to move from what in retrospect seems to have been a pedagogic factory to a more individually based educational situation. This has led to more individual learning and less, or smaller, group teaching, to freer movement within the classroom and to brighter physical surroundings. A symbol of these changes is the fact that desks are no longer bolted to the floor. As a result children may change their position, their classmates, their groupings and may move around more easily. Clearly, different sets of personality traits, particularly concerning how they relate to others, adults or peers, are being encouraged. The moral curriculum has changed to a more individual basis. The so-called contemporary 'open classroom' is organised to build on individual differences and the choices of the individuals within it. The teacher is there to help rather than to direct the individual children concerned.

In the British tradition, largely owing to the way in which the educational system developed under the influence of Arnold, teachers have been seen as responsible for the development of the whole man, both academic and moral. Therefore there has always been a strong element of pastoral care, even in the role of the state school teacher. This element was relatively easy to fulfil when a teacher's role was marked by benevolent authority, but with the move towards greater emphasis upon individual differences, even where class sizes are smaller, teachers have a much more difficult pastoral task. Furthermore where the ethos of the school does not match that of the home, problems increase, especially when there is a tendency for families to pass over some of their formerly accepted functions to the school. These processes have occurred at a time when there has been a considerable growth in the helping professions, that is, of counsellors and therapists, who are experts in assisting individuals in their personal, largely non-physiological, problems. Indeed the greater wealth of society has created both the possibility for such professions and the need for them to try to answer the mental problems apparently implicit in a society characterised by the wider range of choices available when habits are no longer so easily accepted without question. In this situation the role of the teacher in relation to the moral curriculum is subtly changed. His pastoral role is still there, but he no longer is meant to know all the answers. The total man in all his academic and moral aspects is no longer cared for by his class teacher, but by a team, the main member of which is the teacher, through whom other experts may be approached.

The state secondary schools were initially modelled upon the independent schools in which their administrators and controllers had themselves been educated. Their striving for status, as has been seen to be the case in the academic curriculum, led to an emphasis upon competition. Thus originally, and up to the 1950s, when the big expansion in state-provided secondary schooling began, all the organisational marks of the moral curriculum of the independent schools were found: team games, prize days, prefects and the various extracurricular activities considered to develop moral qualities. More recently, however, there has been some tendency to eliminate such activities because of ideological changes outside the schools. Thus self-discipline is thought to be more important than imposed discipline; responsibility for oneself is to be encouraged, whereas the former readiness to intervene in the behaviour of others is now criticised, both because of a wider tolerance of different patterns of behaviour and because of increased doubts about what is to be considered good or bad conduct. In such a climate of opinion the prefect system is not merely not necessary, but will teach lessons opposite to those desired. Furthermore team games are now considered to be of low importance; indeed all games, even those of an individual nature, have tended to be given much less attention in secondary schools of recent years.

There has been an additional and supporting influence at work in this connection, namely the changing view of many teachers about their role. The increase in industrial activity amongst teachers has meant that they have defined more closely the nature of the behaviour expected of them, and extracurricular activities such as games have been excluded from what may necessarily be asked of them. This is not the case amongst teachers in independent schools who still expect, and are expected, to play a full part in various school activities outside classroom hours. In addition, some teachers have come to see competition as the wrong means to use to motivate children since they believe that it brings out unpleasant characteristics in those competing and, worst of all, necessarily implies that as well as winners there will be losers, who may come to see themselves as less able than others in all sorts of ways. Those holding such views will wish to eliminate the competition and hierarchical elements so characteristic of the Arnoldian moral curriculum. Therefore in many state secondary schools today much more emphasis is put upon responsibility for one's own behaviour and on ensuring that all students experience success of some sort rather than upon imposed discipline and competition.

Secondary schools tend to be larger than primary schools and this raises the problem of whether size has any influence on the nature of the moral curriculum taught. Organisational arrangements have been made in large schools to ensure that pastoral care is exercised through a system of form teachers so that no single child's development is not observed. But a case is often put that large schools make more chances available to students, both in academic and extracurricular activities. However evidence from schools both in Australia and in the United States of America indicates that things are not so simple as this (W.J. Campbell, 1971). In work done in high schools both in Brisbane and in Kansas it seemed that the extracurricular programme, seen from the standpoint of the individual student, was far richer in smaller than in larger schools. There may have been a wider range in absolute terms of offerings available to him in the big school, but in the small school the individual student was far more likely to take up a larger number of the narrow range of options given to him. Relatively he was, and seemed to feel, more rooted in the social system of the small school. These findings raise important, and largely as yet unexplored, issues concerning the moral curriculum. The alienation of youth from social systems is seen as general and is felt by many youths themselves in the form of enmity to school, but there is a possibility that secondary schools which are large are, by their size alone, helping to create, at least in part, this serious contemporary moral problem.

Largely in answer to such problems state educational systems have themselves, since about 1970, begun to establish progressive secondary schools. Thus in Victoria a number of so-called 'community schools' have been evolved (P.W. Musgrave and R.J.W. Selleck, 1975). Usually these have been small, so that personal relationships between teachers and students may be close and easy. Such a school as Swinburne Community School, consisting of about one hundred and twenty pupils, aims to allow parents to play a part in the school community and for students to use the community around the school as an educational resource. Furthermore the students play a large part in running the school, hence increasing their sense of being members of a community. Clearly, the word 'community' is used in a number of senses, but here the implication is that the student shall have the experience of being rooted in various social networks so that the possibility of his feeling alienated is diminished and so that he learns a firm moral commitment to others. The vocabulary of motives instilled is non-competitive and tolerant, though in a helpful and committed way, of others. More recently, an attempt was started at Huntingdale Technical School to translate the same ideals into a much larger organisation—a school eventually to be of over nine hundred students. The hope is that this can be achieved by splitting the school up into minischools with their own staff, students and individuality, which will share certain common facilities such as a library, laboratories and sporting facilities—a remarkable extension of the way in which Arnold organised Rugby, but with very different moral aims.

Another tendency amongst community schools relates to the manner of organising the academic curriculum and can be seen in particular at Sydney Road School. Work is on topics, not on subjects, and is planned to lead out into the community around the school. This work is done in groups, not as individuals. Though these methods may have academic implications, more particularly in relation to motivation, it is hoped that the main lesson learnt as a result of the pedagogy adopted will be moral in nature. Co-operation, not competition, with one's peers is stressed. Hierarchy is not emphasised and the authority both of adults and of existing systems of knowledge is open to question. In other words the pedagogy carries a radical moral lesson.

Yet, despite these changes, both in the form of community schools and in the manner in which primary and secondary schools are now carried on, one may note that in Victoria, Regulation XVI of the Education Department's *Regulations, General Instructions and Information* still reads as follows:

2.   Teachers shall do all in their power to form habits of right conduct in their pupils by—
     (i) inculcating the principles of morality, truth and justice;
     (ii) encouraging and judiciously enforcing personal neatness and cleanliness;
     and
     (iii) training the children in habits of modest, orderly and polite behaviour.

It may well be that changes come to the moral curriculum even more slowly than to the academic curriculum.

iii)   The Education of the Sexes. One of the most striking organisational features of our present educational system is the tendency to treat boys and girls differently—even in coeducational establishments. In the past the tendency was that beyond the elementary stage, wherever possible, schools should be single-sex in their intake. This had been, and largely still is, the case in the independent school system, though even here, perhaps because of changing economic, rather than ideological conditions, there is some sign of movement towards coeducation. In the early 1970s, the situation was that 36 per cent of all fourteen-year-olds in Australia were in single-sex schools and 6 per cent of those in coeducational schools were taught separately. At the form six level, 46 per cent were in single-sex schools and 3 per cent of those in coeducational schools were taught separately (*Girls, School & Society*, 1975: 63). Thus between 40 and 50 per cent of all secondary school students are taught in single-sex situations.

Even when students are in coeducational schools they are very often treated so differently that the lessons learnt in single-sex situations are implicit in the coeducational school. For instance, some subjects are sex-typed; an obvious case is Domestic Science, but, as we saw in Table 4.2, Physics for boys, Biology, and even English Literature for girls, are other examples. Several sports are also sex-typed or are played separately; compare football and hockey. Some administrative activities are segregated by sex; thus heavy lifting or cleaning is done by boys, whilst tea-making, flower arrangement and light cleaning is done by girls. Perhaps the most obvious example of such organisational sex-typing has been that very often in coeducational schools there have been separate playgrounds for boys and for girls. In all these ways schools encourage their students to behave according to the accepted sex roles and, since the concept of role is a mutual one, to behave towards each other according to expectations. The moral curriculum has a sexual dimension.

The role of women in Australian society has changed quite considerably during this century. Around 1900 the place of the woman might be seen to be the home, but the proportion of women in the labour force was increasing. Since more women were in domestic service than in any other single occupation, two birds could be killed with one stone if girls were taught Domestic Science; the demand of the middle class for servants and the need for the skills of the home-maker would both be met. From the 1880s in New South Wales and Victoria, Cooking was added to the Needlework already taught in the elementary schools, but the Education Department in Victoria under Tate's influence extended this provision by opening Schools of Domestic Arts for adolescent girls. By the late 1930s, by which time the days of cheap domestic labour had ended and women occupied a wider range of positions in this labour force, Domestic Science was firmly entrenched in the curriculum, but now only with its secondary aim of producing home-makers (B. Bessant, 1976). It is only very recently that boys also have begun to take this subject, under the impact of attempts to end sexual stereotyping in school subjects.

This same movement has drawn attention to the very strong influence in textbooks of the sex-typing of children. Thus in a study of the reading books used at the primary level in New South Wales, both men and women were found to be portrayed as active, independent and knowledgeable, but the women were shown at home whilst the men were allowed to occupy a wider range of positions. In secondary texts women were gentle, timid, conforming, domesticated and fearful under stress; they were shown as occupied as housewives, mothers, nurses, teachers and models. Men, on the other hand, were adventurous, rational, strong, firm and unafraid; they were shown in a wide range of occupations, usually as bread-winner of the family and in dirty and technical tasks (*Girls, School & Society*, 1975: 71–74). There have now been many similar studies. It can be seen that the materials provided in schools carry an important moral lesson concerning sex-typed behaviour.

iv) Sanctions. All such behavioural standards are supported by systems of rewards and punishments. Historically the traditionalists have put much emphasis on the latter and the progressivists on the former. Little is known, even of contemporary conditions, concerning the use of sanctions in schools. Certainly in the nineteenth century independent school physical punishment was reputedly very common and severe. Likewise the system of payment by results seems to have encouraged teachers to punish both physically and by, for example, keeping children in at playtime in order to learn academic work. But physical punishments for moral matters were also common. In a study of English elementary schools during 1900–39 almost one half of physical punishments were for moral, as opposed to academic, offences. About one-tenth of all such punishments were given to girls, and infants, too, were, on occasion, physically punished (P.W. Musgrave, 1978: 91). The rate of corporal punishment declined considerably throughout the years referred to and certainly today in Australia physical punishment in schools is at least *thought* to be rare and this belief also covers independent schools where the practice of prefects administering corporal punishment for minor moral offences has almost ceased. Some relevant evidence is presented in a recent major Australian study that was carried out in Western Australia (*Discipline in Secondary Schools in W.A.*, 1972).

All States allow corporal punishment in certain circumstances, though not for academic offences. In all States detention of students after school is permissible, though in rural areas the departure of buses must limit its usage. Expulsion from school is possible in all States under different circumstances, though this ultimate sanction can really be seen as an admission of failure since the school no longer has the chance to influence the expelled child. In the Western Australian study about two-thirds of those in years eight and nine said that they had received some form of punishment in the first term of 1972, and despite the current belief concerning the diminished use of corporal punishment nearly a half of these students claimed that their most recent punishment had been the cane. The frequency of punishments, particularly amongst boys, was greater for fourteen-year-olds and fifteen-year-olds than amongst older students. The order of frequency of punishments for years seven and eleven were, respectively: suspension (1; 1), note to parent from teacher/head (2; 2), physical punishment (3; 3), private talking to (4; 7), public sarcasm by teacher (5; 10), yard duty (6; 4), sent from classroom (7; 6), detention (8; 5), public lecture by teacher (9; 9) and extra school work (9; 8). However the traditionally severe forms of punishment seem to yield diminishing returns from use. The most caned students were least fearful of it; they merely grew resentful. Similarly, tidying up the yard humiliated rather than reformed those to whom this punishment was given. In addition, half of those punished felt their treatment to have been unfair. The main conclusion from this study would seem to be that in the contemporary ethos the punishments traditionally used in most secondary schools, especially amongst older students, are often not acting as sanctions in the manner intended, perhaps because many of these 'bad' students are too much against school even to be driven to do its bidding.

This conclusion forces us to question what sorts of rewards are in use and whether these in turn operate as is hoped. Those who support the progressive view would aim to plan activities so that children would want to behave according to the standards accepted in the school concerned. The hope would be that where children wanted to do otherwise, reason would be brought to bear by the children and adults involved to resolve possible difficulties. Rewards of praise and loving acceptance would result in there being little need for punishment. In large urban schools, filled with alienated youth, such hopes seem utopian; yet traditional methods of transmitting the moral curriculum also seem, to say the least, inefficient, if not counter-productive.

2. The Place of the Academic Curriculum

Moral lessons may be taught either through the content of or by the methods used to teach the academic curriculum. Rather more attention will be given here to content than to method.

i)   Content. Until the middle of the nineteenth century, one common argument was that ignorance led to crime and moral failure. Furthermore ignorance similarly made the smooth working of democracy impossible. Hence rationality supported by adequate knowledge was needed to ensure a moral, democratic society. Schooling would overcome ignorance and, therefore, help to reduce crime and produce democracy. Under these circumstances the content of the reading books used in schools became an important consideration and material that was seen to be morally uplifting was used to instil ideas of order, respectability and of just reward or retribution for actions undertaken. The social importance of such instruction was emphasised by a Sydney journalist as late as 1893 in these words:

> A moral community of one million should not require one-tenth of our police force with its proportional expenditure.
>
> (A.G. Austin and R.J.W. Selleck, 1975: 281)

Present morality here went hand in hand with *laissez-faire* views on public expenditure.

After federation Australian society had become more confident of itself. The establishment of an egalitarian and democratic social system was nearer at hand. Law and order had replaced the incipient anarchy, as it then seemed, of the Gold Rush era. The focus in the moral curriculum shifted away from the former emphasis upon ensuring conformist qualities in interpersonal behaviour to teaching such political virtues as loyalty to the new country and to the Empire. The old qualities were not ignored, but new material now appeared in the elementary curriculum, often under the heading of Civics, which aimed to ensure political self-control in future citizens.

The development of History as a school subject is pertinent at this point. In Victoria History was introduced into elementary schools in the middle of the last century as an adjunct to Reading. The historical stories used then in the *Royal Readers* have been christened 'drum and trumpet history'. Tales of the deeds of great men, rarely women, from British history were used for Reading lessons with the explicit aim of teaching patriotism, of training future citizens and of developing character. The Jubilees of 1887 and 1897 encouraged this tendency. In 1902 Tate introduced a new syllabus, still about great men, but with a new emphasis on social and Australian history and on Civics rather than, as formerly, on political history; clearly a new type of Australian patriotism and political morality had to be taught. This tendency, initiated by Tate in answer to the spirit of the times, was carried further in the revision of 1934 and especially after World War II. By the 1950s the subject which was now called Social Studies, since it consisted of an amalgamation of History, Geography and Civics, aimed to teach children how to live together, preserving freedom in an increasingly Australia-centred world (A.R. Trethewey, 1974).

We have seen that recently Social Studies has been seen as an ideal source for moral lessons of a progressive nature. There are three main reasons for this. Because of the wide range of material available selection must be made; electives can easily be made available to the students and they can easily begin to learn to make choices. Secondly, students must make decisions about their stances on major social issues and this process inevitably contains a moral element. In addition, because of the integrated nature of the subject matter old ways of thinking about knowledge can be challenged and some aspects of authority seen in a less deferential manner.

The development of Social Studies was more complex than so far described because of the complexities of Australian nationalism. There were two considerable groups, somewhat overlapping, who disagreed with the ruling British view of Australian nationality, namely the Roman Catholics, who tended to take an Irish view of Britain, and the Labor party, who, as noted already, in its more utopian moments viewed the world in international terms. The Roman Catholics in Victoria managed to establish their own separate History courses in 1933. The Labor parties have always wanted to try to ensure a party-less curriculum in schools. Both these tendencies have blurred the version of political morality taught in the Australian schools. Since World War II the process has become further complicated by the immense inflow of migrants of non-British stock. Many such migrants now arrange for their children to attend language classes in the evenings or on Saturday mornings in order to preserve something of their own ethnic culture in this strange country. The textbooks used are brought from the native land and carry the moral curriculum of that country. Thus Greek children, born in Melbourne, attend Victorian schools by day, supposedly learning to live as Australians, and then go to a native language school where, on occasions, the textbooks used had been written for use under the extremely un-democratic regime ruling Greece until recently.

The native tongue is the primary vehicle for carrying the moral assumptions of a nation. Thus an Australian, early in life, learns the meaning of 'fair go', 'mate', or 'bludger', all of which are terms carrying deep national moral meaning. But the relevant school subject, English, has always had two rather different parts to it. The first relates to the teaching of clear expression, both oral and written, in the native tongue. Although this part carries implicit moral meaning the other, the critical study of literature, has always done so in an obvious fashion. Matthew Arnold, son of Thomas, who in addition to being a literary critic and school inspector was a poet, had much influence in this context. We have remarked that he saw schools, especially through the study of poetry, as shedding 'sweetness and light'. But the crucial choice was to be made: which literature? and what sort of 'light'? Clearly, Scott rather than de Sade.

More recently the Cambridge critic, F.R. Leavis, has had a great influence on English teaching in schools. He and his disciples have emphasised that the practice of literary criticism at any level is involved with disentangling the values implicit in the works under examination. Only when evaluative criteria are used can the decision be made that a writer is great. The parents to whom reference was made earlier in this chapter intuitively felt this when they objected to the study by adolescents of such works as *Catcher in the Rye*. Leavis's methods, however, have been pushed beyond the study of literature. It is possible in much the same way to examine critically the environment, thereby uncovering the values at work in, for example, advertising, the mass media, or the process of industrialisation. So it is that much of the work done under the name 'English' has come to be the teaching to students of how to examine the values at work in society, and particularly the doing so from the standpoint that urbanisation and industrialisation have been accompanied by a definite decline in moral standards.

More recently, since about 1960, the increase of wealth per capita in many advanced societies including Australia has also allowed the questioning of the values underpinning the Protestant Ethic and the capitalist system itself. These are the moral values that are the mainspring of our present economic system. Some now ask: why work? why try to 'get out'? why save? These changes have paralleled a decline in the belief of absolute moralities and the growth of a more relativistic position. Tolerance of individuals of very different natures is now accepted. Thus the disentangling of the values involved in various positions that are now allowable, but that were once morally forbidden—'shacking up' has replaced 'living in sin'—is essential if an adolescent is to make wise choices on leaving school and, as has been the case since literature was studied in schools, sensitive teachers of English can help in this part of the moral curriculum.

Such choices extend beyond the skills of interpersonal life with which English has come to deal. Many choices that have moral implications also demand scientific knowledge if the process of choosing is to lead to wise decisions after consideration of the relevant issues. Thus, Health Education can deal with such aspects of social living as marriage, family life, sexual behaviour, drugs and mental illness. Some of these topics can also be covered in Domestic Science lessons. Styles of expenditure can be studied here or in Consumer Education, which, leading in full circle, can also be taught in such a manner that the way the capitalist system is now operating can be criticised. In all these cases a further point should be noted. All deal with topics that formerly were thought to be the responsibility of the family. Again, we may note that the moral curriculum of the school grows as that of the family diminishes.

Games and Physical Education have always been seen by educators as an important source of moral lessons. Originally physical training in the elementary schools took the form of drill with clear implications for obedience, conformity and deference. When Games entered the school curriculum they were almost always in the form of team games. The emphasis was to be on the learning of co-operation, team spirit, putting others before self, the competitive spirit, taking defeat well, as much as, if not more than, such individual qualities as perseverance, taking hard knocks, or personal fitness. Periods of national emergency have tended to bring increasing emphasis to this area of the curriculum. During the recriminations over the near-defeat of the Boer War and during the two world wars Physical Education has been rated highly, but during the depression the federal grants which, for reasons of defence, had been given for training specialist teachers, were withdrawn. During the interwar years there was a gradual movement towards more games and less drill.

Since World War II Games have become a less important part of the school curriculum in all Australian schools, even in the independent schools, where so much emphasis had always been put upon them and upon the moral lessons it was believed were learnt from them. Furthermore in line with the move away from competition and towards individual development, the range of games played has widened to allow swimming, tennis, squash and athletics, all more individualistic in character than the formerly provided range of team games. In addition, in some schools activities other than Games are now available for choice during the relevant timetable periods. Thus students may undertake some form of social service or the Duke of Edinburgh's Award. The moral qualities involved are believed, by those planning the school curriculum, to be similar, and the nature of the activities involved is felt to be more in line with the contemporary ethos.

ii) Method. The very manner in which teachers operate in the classroom is also relevant to moral learning. A comparative study, made in the mid-1960s, of teaching styles in four countries, including Australia, provides some evidence.

> Australians de-emphasize personal relations, free communication, the use of differentiated groups and permissiveness. Adding to the somewhat traditional impression is the fact that two items ranked high were: subject matter and prescriptive rules.
>
> (R.S. Adams, 1970: 54)

This judgement is based on evidence gathered before many of the more recent trends reported here had really influenced teachers. Nevertheless it warns us that we must not forget that many Australian classrooms are very different from those in the few Victorian progressive schools mentioned earlier. Though there is undoubtedly a more liberal spirit in schools than in, say, 1939, yet most classrooms are marked by a mixture of methods with a tendency, according to the teacher's ideology and approach, towards the traditional rather than the progressive style or vice versa. Yet in their pure form each of these styles has clear moral lessons for pupils. The traditional style, alluded to in the quotation as the norm, encourages a ready obedience and deference to the authority of the teacher in both academic and moral matters; the teacher operates on a group and consensual basis so that agreement is emphasised and conflict discouraged. A progressive teacher, however, encourages individuality, differences, challenges to himself and to the present basis of knowledge; creativity and self-responsibility are the key qualities that are to be developed.

Much attention has lately been given by those who analyse classroom interaction to the ways in which teachers attach labels to pupils which are then internalised by them as permanent traits of personality. Usually the labels considered have related to cleverness or its lack, but moral as well as cognitive labels are applied to students in the classroom. Thus a teacher can create a moral scapegoat—'Not John Smith again!'. Morally positive labels, for example of being 'creative', also may be applied to students—'Listen to Sue's poem'. The ways in which such moral labels are applied, come to be believed and to be held permanently are very subtle. The teacher may isolate one student, selectively ignore another, place others in a special part of the classroom, or touch students in particular ways at certain times; such apparently small details of interaction seem to play a part in the process.[1] Certainly it would seem to be important in the case of morally *negative* labels to apply them to acts, not persons, so that there is less chance of the student permanently learning a trait, whilst in the case of morally *positive* labels the person may be so labelled as the intention is to teach the child some positively evaluated characteristic.

Attempts have been made, in various ways and for various reasons, to reduce the status differential in the classroom between teacher and taught. Students are encouraged to call the teacher by his christian name; teachers have mixed with students outside the school on trips, in games and at adventure camps. Many of these methods have long been used by teachers in the independent schools when organising extracurricular activities, though it should be noted that symbolically these attempts to come closer to pupils have usually been made off the school premises. Furthermore such methods of teaching raise considerable problems in the case of many migrant groups for whom the authority of the teacher is absolutely inviolate. In such cases, the gap between school and home may be increased rather than diminished by the style of teaching used.

3. Extracurricular Activities

Much has always been made of extracurricular activities in the independent schools. Games have already been mentioned, but a large range of clubs has also been encouraged. The aims were twofold, firstly that certain interests might be learnt that would last throughout life and, secondly, that additional activities would be available in which the moral qualities of leadership and service might be learnt.

---

1. T.D. Evans, Creating Creativity: A Sociological Study of Early School Socialisation, unpublished Ph.D. thesis, Monash University, 1978.

Leadership training was a concept once much spoken of in relation to secondary schools. The prefect system, for example, was often seen in this connection. Modern social psychology has failed to find one generic trait which might be termed 'Leadership', but has indicated that various social groups demand different qualities in their leaders. The industrial entrepreneur, the research scientist, the headmaster and the trade union official—each need differing traits to sustain them in their positions. In view of this new perspective on leadership the availability of a wide range of positions in any school becomes important if that school aims to allow its students to realise what their potentialities as leaders might be.

As early as the 1950s R.F. Butts noted that in Australian schools, except for sports, extracurricular activities were not given much importance. For the reasons referred to earlier in this chapter this is probably truer in the 1970s; and even sports have a lesser role now in schools, though maybe not in Australian society as a whole. Despite the fact that there is an undoubted feeling in Australia that tall poppies should be cut down, there does seem to be a case for providing as many opportunities as possible for students to experiment, whilst some moral 'failure' is still condoned, so that they may more fully know their own moral qualities before entering the adult world. This view reinforces the need for the presence of a wide range of extracurricular activities as part of the moral curriculum of any school.

Furthermore the apparent lack of extracurricular activities outside the independent schools may also be criticised in relation to the first aim for such opportunities, namely that of developing lifelong interests in students. As the number of hours worked in the labour force per week falls, and perhaps also because the number of those unemployed continues to present an apparently intractable problem, there would seem to be a strong case for schools giving much attention to the preparation of their students for this future leisure time. Schools do have different ways of tackling this task; some stress future work before future leisure, others more nearly put equal emphasis on both aims; others, again, and perhaps in the Australian utilitarian tradition this is the majority, still educate for work, not for leisure.

One other very important extracurricular activity for boys has always been the Cadet Corps. The first such units were established in New South Wales in the mid-1860s. After federation, control of the Cadets passed from the States to the Commonwealth and by the Defence Act of 1910, not repealed in this respect until 1929, there was supposed to be universal military training for all boys between fourteen and eighteen who were medically fit. By 1973 the aims of Army School Cadet training were said to be 'to develop qualities of leadership, citizenship and self-reliance in a framework of military activities'. Out of 1,940 secondary schools catering for boys in Australia 312 (16 per cent) had Cadet units, 201 (64.4 per cent) of which were in state schools. A total of about 35,000 boys were involved in Cadet activities (*Report on the Army Cadet Corps*, 1974). In 1975 the Australian Government withdrew almost all financial aid from these Corps so that very few schools now continue to maintain them. Some persons have always been opposed to military activities of this nature, but have felt that a similarly disciplined framework within which many of the same moral lessons would be learnt by both boys and girls could be supplied by the presence of a Scout or Guide troop.

4. Conclusion

The Australian moral curriculum, or selection of the moral culture to be transmitted to the next generation, has been constrained by much the same set of institutional forces as the Australian academic curriculum. Economic and political circumstances clearly have affected the way in which it has developed first in colonial and then in Australian schools. So also has the changing salience of the family in the Australian social structure. But for two reasons ideological changes are perhaps here more influential than in the case of the academic curriculum. Firstly, morality depends upon what set of values is rated high, both by those who control the educational system and, in a democracy, by the voters to whom the controllers must ultimately bow, and this, in turn, is much under the influence of ideological change. Thus the movement from a more absolute to a more relativistic morality has had an effect on moral teaching in schools. Changes in the interpretation of Australian nationalism have clearly affected the moral content of the academic curriculum. The new feminism has influenced both school organisation, and the content and method of teaching academic subjects, so that the standards taught in relation to behaviour between the sexes have changed. The growth of a more individualistic perspective on life has had an effect on the way Games and Physical Education are taught in schools and, as a result, the moral lessons that it is hoped will be learnt are now very different from even fifty years ago.

But, secondly, ideological changes that concern morality both affect and are deeply important to parents and others interested in the schools so that, whereas the academic curriculum is usually seen as beyond their competence, they are felt to be, and do feel themselves to be, expert in moral matters. Teachers, then, who teach a morality that is seen as outside the tolerated range will often be brought to book and those in control of the schools will have to listen to the complaints of those who feel the moral teaching to be deviant. An independent school that teaches a deviant morality, even where this is called progressive education, must pay its way economically. A state school that tries to do the same raises political problems for those running the educational system; those in power or the administrators who work for them will have either to forestall such difficulties by not allowing deviant teaching to begin or to bring erring teachers back within the agreed range of tolerated morality.

One last point may be made. The moral curriculum, in a way that parallels the changes in the academic curriculum described in the last two chapters, has moved from a formal, clear and more or less agreed set of precepts to a pluralist morality within which choice is possible. The meaning of the moral situation for the individual involved is what now matters, so that students cannot now be programmed with the recipes to solve their future moral problems. They need, or so many believe, to be given practice in reflection on the differing contexts and moralities which they may meet in the rapidly changing contemporary world. In moral, as well as academic, matters the curriculum has moved towards Beeby's stage of Meaning.

Bibliography

HANSEN, I.V. (1971): *Nor Free Nor Secular*. Oxford University Press: Melbourne. A pioneer study of the organisation and operation of six Victorian independent schools.

MUSGRAVE, P.W. (1978): *The Moral Curriculum*. Methuen: London. Though mainly concerning Britain, an account of the development of and social factors influencing moral education.

Discipline in Secondary Schools in Western Australia (1972): Education Department of W.A.: Perth. The report of an investigation, including a questionnaire study amongst students, into all aspects of discipline in W.A. secondary schools.

Girls, School & Society (1975): Report of a Study Group to the Schools Commission: Canberra. A wide-ranging account, based on bringing together existing research on various aspects of the position of girls in schools.

Other References

ADAMS, R.S. (1970): 'Perceived Teaching Style', *Comparative Education Review*, 14 (1) 50–59.

BESSANT, B. (1976): 'Domestic Science Schools and Women's Place', *Australian Journal of Education*, 20 (1) 1–9.

CAMPBELL, W.J. (1971): 'Some Effects of Size and Organisation of Secondary Schools on the Experience of Pupils in Extra-curricular Behaviour Settings', in Campbell, W.J., ed., *Scholars in Context*. Wiley: Sydney.

FITZGERALD, R.T., MUSGRAVE, P.W. and PETTIT, D.W. (1976): *Participation in Schools?* A.C.E.R.: Hawthorn (Vic.).

HIMMELWEIT, H.T. and SWIFT, B., (1969): 'A Model for the Understanding of the School as a Socializing Agency', in Mussen, P.H., Langer, J. and Covington, M., eds, *Trends and Issues in Developmental Psychology*. Holt, Rinehart & Winston: New York.

TRETHEWEY, A.R., (1974): 'Social and Educational Influences on the Definition of a Subject: History in Victoria', in Musgrave, P.W., ed., *Contemporary Studies in the Curriculum*. Angus & Robertson: Sydney.

TURNEY, C. (1967): 'The Advent and Adaptation of the Arnold Public School Tradition in New South Wales. II', *Australian Journal of Education* 11 (1).

Report on the Army Cadet Corps (1974): Committee of Inquiry into C.M.F., Australian Government Publishing Service: Canberra.

6. *Curricular Change: Some Conclusions*

> We must not forget that nothing tends to become more easily stereotyped and prone to decay than any academic procedure whatsoever.

(E. Durkheim, 1977: 142)

In the past three chapters the concepts and framework developed in Chapter 2 have been used to outline the development of curriculum in Australian schools with the aim of highlighting the social factors that were influential in this process. The curriculum itself has been considered analytically from three perspectives.

Firstly, it has been seen as a social phenomenon that is dependent upon social forces whose influence cannot be avoided by those responsible for determining its nature. In this way we have seen that, for example, the salience of the economy since the late nineteenth century and the recent ideological shift towards radical individualism have affected curricular content. For many people a major problem has been the difficulty so vividly indicated in the quotation from Durkheim at the head of this chapter, namely that the content of the curriculum becomes taken for granted and change in it lags behind what many consider would meet the present needs of certain sections of society.

Secondly, we have examined the curriculum as a social phenomenon that intervenes between an agent of change and an effect. Thus, for various reasons, curricular changes were made around 1900 in Victoria that had the effect of strengthening the unequal distribution of knowledge between the social classes. Again, since about 1970 research has shown that the present organisation of the curriculum presents a different view of the world to boys and to girls. In both these cases the curriculum analytically stands between some cause and an effect. The problem here is that ideological changes seem difficult to predict and, therefore, there is the ever-present likelihood that some new disadvantage will be discovered in the way in which knowledge is being managed through the curriculum. Since, as just indicated, the curriculum tends to resist change, there is once again a problem of how to shift the educational system in the desired direction.

Finally, the curriculum may be seen as an independent source of change in the social system itself. We have seen, for example, that demands have been made upon teachers of English and Social Studies that they inculcate a sceptical spirit in relation to advertising in order that consumers may not be so easily exploited. The intention here is that by changing curricula a new social reality may be created outside the school. Once again, the whole process depends upon the initial change taking place in the school.

In each of the three stances that we have used, therefore, there has been an assumption that change would occur in schools, but we have as yet not really examined how such changes do in fact take place. The focus in this chapter, therefore, will be upon change itself and not its sources. The problem will be tackled under two headings: planned change and reflective change. Planned change will be taken to refer to change planned outside individual schools, whereas reflective change will be used to cover cases where change is initiated at the school level.

1. Planned Change

i) Historical. Before 1945 the ideological climate and the accepted method of control of Australian educational systems was such that, at least in theory, change was rather simple to achieve. There was little opposition to the authority of the expert or of the man, and it invariably was a male, higher up the hierarchy. Thus if a change in the curriculum was to be made, it was initiated in the upper echelons of the Education Department, promulgated through official channels and change invariably followed in the schools, though inspectors might not be able to check every small deviation. The situation in secondary schools, certainly before the 1920s, was somewhat different since schools were largely not provided by the States and were, therefore, outside the control of the Education Department. In these schools the curriculum was controlled by those who traditionally held authority over academic knowledge, the universities; this control was achieved by means of the matriculation examination and certain other external examinations set at levels prior to year twelve. The situation in both primary and secondary schools, therefore, expressed in a simplified form, was that the controllers decided, the administration implemented and the teachers, who had on the whole not been consulted, acted. At that date no one would have considered asking the students or even their parents, since they had neither the expertise seen as necessary nor, perhaps more importantly, had they any power in this respect.

It was in this way that the various alterations to the curriculum of the elementary school were made during the time of payment by result. Around 1900 the paternalism became a little more benevolent in that the opinions of some teachers were sought occasionally and in that, as in the case of the Fink and Knibbs-Turner Commissions, data was gathered from other sources, for example, employers, upon which more apt decisions could be made. Furthermore, the ultimate decisions about curricula and their implementation had to depend upon the political skills of such administrators as Tate and Board, who had the opportunities to press forward in directions that interested them or to raise questions when they were in opposition to certain developments. Thus, for instance, Board tried to introduce an element of progressive primary education and Tate had initially to introduce secondary education into Victoria by rather backdoor routes.

However, by the interwar years, although the skills of political manipulation will always remain a constant in achieving change, curricular or otherwise, two new factors had to be considered. There was, firstly, the new trust in educational theory and research. Therefore, as in the case of the new Victorian elementary school curriculum of 1934, considerable prior thought was given to the whole theoretical basis of the proposed changes by G.S. Browne and others and this was done in relation to similar curricula in Britain and the United States of America. Furthermore the proposals were also discussed with teachers and tested prior to publication. Paternalism had been modified and had become more scientific in its basis. Certainly the process, in part because it was more thorough, was more complex in that more options were opened up and more interests taken into account. Hence changes that were acceptable to all were now hard to achieve.

Since 1945 such paternalistic change is more rarely found in relation to the Australian curriculum, and the obvious, though not the only, examples of it relate to secondary science curricula. Physics is an interesting case. A version of the Physical Sciences Study Committee (PSSC) course, developed in the United States, was adopted in the late 1960s in Victoria, Western Australia and Queensland for use in years eleven and twelve, that is basically for external examination work. In Victoria considerable efforts were made to prepare teachers and to help them in the new courses. Meanwhile in New South Wales under the Wyndham scheme new Physics courses were introduced largely without trials and with little involvement of teachers; these courses have been a constant source of controversy (G.A. Ramsey, 1972: 4–5). Thus, just prior to the great growth of teacher militance in Victorian secondary schools, a major curricular change planned by experts on behalf of the universities was speedily and successfully introduced by the local examinations board; much of the success of this operation must be put down to the careful way in which the teachers concerned were consulted and their problems taken into account.

ii)   The Concept of the Curriculum Project. In the United States of America, after the Russians launched Sputnik in 1957, there was a realisation, almost of panic proportions, that science and mathematics teaching and curricula had lagged behind the needs of a society whose economy and defence potential rested in a very fundamental way upon the natural sciences and mathematics. The immediate result was the concentration of the development of curricula in Physics, Chemistry, Biology and Mathematics in a number of large-scale projects. Ultimately the concept of curriculum renewal and the methods adopted in the sciences spread to other school subjects, first of all to the modern languages, also seen as subjects of national importance, and then to various branches of the humanities, for example, English and Social Studies.

The new method relied upon a large team made up of academic experts, who could advise what material from all the most up-to-date knowledge should be selected as relevant for the purpose on hand; of those with experience in teaching, who could bring their practical knowledge and skills to the preparation of new materials and the writing of new texts; and of practising teachers who would test the new curriculum and its related materials in their classrooms. The administration and control of such a team over the three or four years that was found to be the minimum necessary to produce a course for, perhaps, one school year in one branch of science proved to be very costly. In some cases the hope was that when the new materials were published they would be bought by so many schools that the original outlay could be paid back, and even that where commercial publications were involved a profit would be made. Many of the new materials relied upon such aids as films or photographs of high quality and were put out as kits or split into several separate units rather than taking the old form of one textbook so that clearly the place and work of educational publishers was also much changed.

Initially Australia was influenced in two ways by this new method of developing curricula. The first effect was that various States or schools adopted some of the individual new projects in a more or less unchanged form. Thus, as noted, PSSC was widely adopted in Australia. In addition, materials developed by the English Schools Council, for example, those connected with the Humanities Project, were adopted. One interesting variation on direct adoption was the taking up in Australia of the United States Biological Sciences Curriculum Study (BSCS) materials, *Web of Life,* which had first to be adapted to Australian flora and fauna. Ultimately a team rewrote the United States material under the auspices of the Australian Academy of Science who published the new version at minimum cost for schools, though they were also able to earn considerable funds for themselves, since Biology, as we have seen, turned out to be a subject that grew rapidly in popularity in schools. A further point about BSCS in Australia is that machinery has been kept in being to revise the materials on a regular basis—a provision not usual since project teams are normally dispersed once the materials for which they have been created have been published.

The second effect in Australia, namely the establishment of the CDC, was indirect and slower to come about, owing something to English example: in 1964 the Schools Council was established to be responsible for the development of curricula in England and Wales. After some initial distrust amongst both teachers and local authorities, who believed that such a body might lead to centralised control of the curriculum the Schools Council initiated a number of now well-known large scale curricular developments over a wide range of subjects and at both primary and secondary levels. The establishment of a similar body in Australia was hamstrung by the need to involve all States, each of which in any case already had a variously named curriculum and research branch within its Education Department. As in the United States of America the breakthrough came in the field of science. In Victoria, as a result of reports of what was happening in the United States, a local project, the Junior Secondary Science Project (JSSP) was funded in 1966 under the auspices of ACER and VUSEB. The resulting materials were also adopted in some schools in neighbouring States so that, when JSSP terminated in 1969, an approach could be made to the Commonwealth Government by ACER on behalf of Victoria, South Australia and Tasmania for funds to complete the programme begun by JSSP. Eventually all six States were involved and funds were granted by the Commonwealth on a number of conditions, one of which was that no State would prescribe the materials developed for use in its schools. This project, the Australian Science Education Project (ASEP), ultimately developed forty-seven units for years seven to ten during the period 1969 to 1973.

Before showing how this pioneer co-operative effort by the States to develop materials was followed by the establishment of the Curriculum Development Centre, a centralised body which can be compared in some ways with the English Schools Council, some comments on the diffusion of ASEP materials must be made, because the results are indicative of the problems and rate of take-up of materials from similar large scale, costly projects in Britain and the United States of America. The materials were used more frequently in South Australia and Tasmania than in Queensland and Western Australia, with the other two States falling between these groups. It is worth noting that in Tasmania schools were provided, free, with a choice of ten sets of ASEP materials and that in Western Australia there was a strong commitment, especially in government schools, to the local Curriculum Branch's syllabuses. By February 1976 about 30 per cent of Australian secondary schools still had bought no ASEP units and, on average, ASEP units were used for less than one school term in each of the junior secondary grades (J.H. Owen and R.P. Tisher, 1978). Thus, despite the impossibility of prescription in the case of ASEP and the minimal support given to promotion of the materials through, for example, in-service courses, a fair depth of penetration had been achieved. The very difficult judgement that always has to be made in these large-scale projects is whether the high costs of producing *and* promoting the resultant materials can be afforded. Furthermore in Australia the issue is clouded, not only by the presence of much overseas competition in the field, but also because each State has its own source for similar curricular development work.

One other national project is worth mentioning. In 1967 the National Advisory Committee for UNESCO organised a seminar at Burwood Teachers College, Melbourne, on 'The Teaching of Social Sciences at Secondary Level'. As a result, in 1970 a National Committee on Social Science Teaching was established under Commonwealth funding with State Advisory Committees in each State. This body used a suitable armoury of techniques to develop materials.

National conferences were held; the State Advisory Committees initiated various activities—in Victoria, for example, materials were developed, tested and published, and a system was established of consultants who were practising teachers available to advise other teachers on the job; in addition, in each State a project officer was appointed to encourage this subject (C.B. Tonkin, 1975). In the early 1970s there were similar national committees operating, though perhaps not on such a wide range of activities, in the fields of English Teaching and Asian Studies.

iii)   The Curriculum Development Centre. Clearly these developments meant that more permanent initiatives at a national level were now possible in curricular work in Australia. Interstate jealousies seemed to be diminishing. Thus it was not surprising that one of the early Cabinet decisions of the first Whitlam ministry, announced in June, 1974, was that a national Curriculum Development Centre (CDC) would be established. Though the CDC was soon in interim operation it was not finally established by statute until July 1975. The Centre's functions are set out in the Act and cover a wide range, including activities involved with the development of school curricula and materials, relevant research, the supply of materials, the collection and dissemination of information in this field, and the publication of materials. The CDC has taken over the three National Committees and has followed English precedent in adopting the policy that teachers should be involved in development as much as possible; in addition, the hope is that parents and pupils may also be involved.

The CDC has come to the field of curricular development comparatively late and can build on the lessons of both the United States large scale projects and of the English version of centralised control of large-scale development projects. These projects have not a good record of dissemination, as was shown above in the case of ASEP, which could be said to be a relatively successful example in this respect. Simultaneously with the growth of these big curricular projects there has been the increasing tendency to give schools and teachers greater freedom to develop or choose their own curricula and materials. This trend has been ideologically based in the growing distrust of authority and of university-based prescriptions and in the demand for professional freedom for teachers.

It is, therefore, not surprising that the CDC has taken a very broad range of initiatives. It has invested $1.2m in one large nationwide project, the Social Education Materials Project (SEMP), based on an initiative from the relevant National Committee. It has also financed a number of smaller-scale projects, undertaken in one State or by one worker. In addition, it has also made grants of a few hundred dollars, through the National Committees to individual teachers who might, for example, want to create their own materials specific to one school. The CDC has established study groups on, for example, Curriculum Evaluation, Mathematics Education, and Support Systems for School-Based Curriculum Development. It has begun to set up the mechanisms to disseminate information and, finally, has run conferences on curriculum development (CDC Annual Report, 1975–76).

Clearly, major changes have occurred in the manner in which curriculum planning is carried out in Australia. There has been a movement from massive prescription by state Education Departments and university examination boards to much option at the primary level and minimal prescription, largely at year twelve, at the secondary level. More scientific methods are now used to develop curricula and related materials. Initially this was symbolised in large costly projects, but even with the help of commercial publishers, who naturally wished to maximise their own profits, diffusion has been less successful than was hoped. Thus, when Australia followed England's example and established a national body in this field, we see that the CDC has wisely opted for a multi-faceted approach in its acknowledged task of reaching the teachers in the schools who nowadays, unlike in the past, can make most of the ultimate decisions concerning what selection of knowledge shall be taught.

2. The Reflective Approach

i) Theory. We know very little at all about the type of school environment which encourages curricular innovation. We can, however, learn from various studies, largely made overseas, what factors are characteristic of those teachers who accept curricular innovations soon after they have been developed. Four relevant points can be made which would seem to have importance for any consideration of school-based decisions about curricular change in that they enable us to spot more easily where innovatory teachers may exist within the educational system.

In the first place work done on the successful diffusion of agricultural and medical innovations has been replicated in the educational field and shows that one can identify a certain type of teacher who will probably be relatively keen to experiment with new curricula. He is more likely to be young, more highly qualified than average, to carry high professional status with his colleagues and, finally, to be situated within easy reach of a university or college.

However, secondly, there is little doubt that even teachers of this type are often loath to make changes because of the costs to themselves of upsetting the *status quo*. The problem is not only the individual one that there are psychological blocks to making changes in all of us, but social factors are also at work so that any member of a group who makes or even suggests a change is seen to be threatening the accepted habits and the peace of mind of his colleagues. These social costs of overcoming group defensiveness are the more easily borne by an individual if he has support from one or more colleagues who are either sympathetic to him or also committed to the same curricular change. Thus an evaluation of the English Schools Council Primary Science Project has shown that continued use of an innovation after adoption was more likely if two or more of the teachers in a school were involved in the change.

Thirdly, those involved in disseminating new curricula often fail to realise that the various parties involved have different interests in taking part in curricular experiment. Shipman (1975) has described how, in a project developing an integrated Humanities curriculum for the Schools Council, there were at least three sets of views governing co-operation and, furthermore, that these views changed through time as the project advanced. Local administrators initially wanted to defend their teachers against possible exploitation by the team, but eventually ceased to worry since they judged that nothing revolutionary was going to eventuate; the team members set out with an interest in integration of different school subjects, but ultimately came to emphasise the production of materials, seen as the outcome of the process by which they would themselves finally be judged; the teachers were originally keen to take part in what they thought would be a co-operative venture in producing materials which must then be of use to them, but their interest inevitably waned when the team, largely because of the shortage of time before results had to be achieved, began to make decisions by themselves. Successful diffusion demands attention be paid to the benefits for all the parties concerned at every moment of the developmental process.

Finally, and in extension of the last point, teachers have been shown to have a very different perspective on curricular needs and the manner of their achievement compared with theorists in this field. Teachers have to cope with the day-to-day toil at the chalk-face. They, therefore, are closely attuned to the practical interests of their pupils rather than to the translation of aims and objectives into carefully devised curricular units. Therefore, for most classroom teachers, even those who are well read in educational theory, if a curricular innovation is to be accepted it must have a fairly obvious and immediate appeal to the interests of their pupils as well as to the self-interest of the teacher, or preferably teachers, concerned.

ii) Practice. Because this is an era in which much support is given, particularly amongst those in schools, to the concept of participation by teachers in decisions about what they teach, the emphasis in curricular change has now come to be put much more on reflective decisions than on centrally planned determination. The strategy of those in power in educational systems is now more usually to encourage a rational choice amongst the many available options available to serving teachers, one of which may be the creation on the job of a new curriculum and relevant materials. Such a policy demands certain qualities from teachers. They must know what is available and must be cognisant of the principles involved in curricular planning so that they are competent either to make wise choices or to take their own curricular initiatives. Since most serving teachers at present are not in this position there is the need to give them support so that they are able to make wise and proper curricular decisions.

The type of support that is acceptable to teachers must largely depend upon their present views concerning who should be their agents of curricular respectability. Recent work by Rice amongst Victorian teachers is relevant.[1] Primary teachers were found to be neutral in their attitude towards those connected with universities as a legitimate source of new ideas in the field of curriculum. They were, however, favourable towards subject associations, their peers, inspectors and the Curriculum and Research Branch, though in this last case they retained the right to decide whether to modify or even whether to use the new ideas or not. Only in one subject were these primary teachers unequivocally willing to accept ideas from the traditional centralised sources and this was Mathematics, an area in which, as already noted, many teachers lack basic knowledge and are, therefore, uncertain of themselves. Junior secondary teachers, of both humanities and science subjects, had much the same set of attitudes except that these Victorian secondary teachers were definitely opposed to inspectors as being a legitimate source of new curricular ideas.

1. A.M. Rice, Planned Change, Organisational Innovations and Patterns of Implementation with Particular Reference to the Curriculum, unpublished Ph.D. thesis, Monash University, 1978.

The situation would then seem to be that serving teachers today, especially at the secondary level, may now rarely accept the traditional sources of curricular ideas, but that they are not perhaps as fully competent as is necessary either to make wise choices amongst the now wider range of curricular options or themselves to take the required initiatives in this field. There is, therefore, the need to give teachers the maximum support in these respects. Four approaches would seem apt to enable teachers to reflect more wisely concerning the direction of curricular change.

On a number of occasions in recent years Hoyle (1976) has laid stress upon the 'professionality' of the teaching force. By using this concept he is emphasising that those who wish to be considered as members of a fully professionalised occupation must be marked by great knowledge, which they will keep up to date, and by a trained competence in the fields of knowledge relevant to their own occupation. In this last respect teachers will then not only need to know, for example, about recent research findings in their own subjects, but also how the presently accepted paradigms of their subjects may be translated into school curricula. Since the majority of teachers, apart from the innovators to whom reference was made earlier, are very averse to help from experts from outside the schools, steps have to be taken to allow these innovators and others to whom teachers will listen to influence them. This can be most easily done on the school premises, for example, at special curriculum days. Particularly important is the place of peer consultants who, since they are acceptable to their fellow teachers, can move between schools diffusing information about new practices. These consultants are more likely to be early innovators and, therefore, more closely in touch with such sources of innovation as colleges and universities. In addition, teachers have been found eager to organise training seminars for themselves in teachers' centres. Such organisations have been established in both Britain and Australia to cater for all the schools in a district and often provide the facilities of a discussion centre, supported by a library and technical facilities, so that new ideas can be converted into actual curricular materials, tested and discussed by other teachers, all of whom are facing similar problems. The rationale behind such centres is that they are run by and for teachers themselves to meet their own immediate problems. The disadvantage to such a way of encouraging professionally based change is that the group forces that emerge may, under some circumstances, be harnessed to the uncritical, because unknowledgeable, support of badly planned curricula.

Individual teachers, therefore, should also be given encouragement to act as curricular pioneers, whose ideas and achievements can be fed into existing social networks. This is already being achieved to some extent by means of small grants made available to serving teachers to develop projects at the school level; these have been made available through the CDC and through the somewhat similar Innovations Grants of the Schools Commission. In such programmes fellow teachers are often involved in helping applicants present their proposals in an acceptable manner so that once again peer group forces are involved. However one disadvantage to such largely individually based projects is that the dissemination of the eventual results has proved hard to achieve.

This difficulty leads us to the fourth approach, namely the skilful use of publicity to communicate curricular suggestions and to allow those who make them to earn a little professional status. There are few recognised methods of communicating to peers about professional pedagogical matters in Australia. Academics have journals in which they report and read about recent research findings, but there are very few ways by which teachers can tell their colleagues about innovatory curricular developments. There is, for example, no large circulation journal of the level of *The Times Educational Supplement* in Australia. Until World War II the various Education Department Gazettes did, in small part, carry out this function by publishing small articles on curricular matters, though this channel seems now closed and the new journals run by several of the Departments do not seem to have filled the gap. Various news sheets have begun to evolve, often run by specific professional assocations, but means of publicity on curricular matters are scarce. Yet one should also remember that, even were the means available, there is no guarantee that teachers would read such material. Indeed there are a number of research reports based on work both in the United States of America and Britain that show the teachers in these countries to have poor records in this respect.

The suggestion that is being made here is that in the present ideological climate, characterised as it is by individualism and antiauthoritarianism, planned curricular change of the old centralised type is not acceptable to teachers. They wish to operate on a reflective basis though many admit that they are not fully competent to do so. Hence those responsible for running educational systems must provide supports that make the necessary information and facilities available to teachers both as individuals and in groups. The curricular innovators will themselves seek out the necessary knowledge, but the majority of practising teachers do not do so, hence the need for support. But the channels used must be those seen as legitimate by contemporary teachers. Thus under present circumstances there is need to provide serving teachers with in-service facilities so that they can become competent to judge the worth, for their purposes, of curricular suggestions and materials developed by teams or publishers, are able to put into operation their own new ideas and, finally, are in a position easily to hear of curricular suggestions which may be of use to them. In this way the reflective approach to curricular change will become based on the maximum possible relevant skills and knowledge.

3. Conclusion

In this chapter we have been considering the actual process whereby changes in curriculum occur in schools. Formerly, this process was rather simple; change took place because teachers were told to do something different. This was justifiable when teachers were not well trained and at the elementary level had usually not undertaken much secondary education. More recently, except at the higher levels of the secondary schools, curricular direction has become unacceptable. Indeed many teachers, certainly in primary schools, have now a sufficient foundation of knowledge upon which to base most curricular decisions, but the skills of converting innovatory ideas into actual curricula and related materials are, perhaps, still scarce. The situation can once again be described in Beeby's terminology as a movement from the Formal stage towards one of Meaning, though the full basis of understanding may not yet be available to all practising teachers.

Therefore where change is deemed necessary, and this chapter should not be read as an appeal for change for change's sake, there is a need for establishing a number of mechanisms which will rely upon existing social forces. Those in control of schools will, thereby, rely on the rewards of self-esteem that a professional sees worth seeking through the support systems made available to the teachers in schools. It is extremely unlikely that the new curricula that will emerge in the schools will add to academic knowledge since teachers still tend to rely very heavily upon the universities for their basis of knowledge. Teachers will, however, play a much more active role in the selection of the academic knowledge that is made available to the various categories of students that those in schools decide to treat differently. However the moral curriculum is another matter. Each school has the opportunity to arrange a very different set of approved social behaviours, though, even here, as indicated in the last chapter, parents and others in the local environment who are interested in the school may act to restrict innovatory aspects of the moral curriculum.

Bibliography

HOYLE, E. (1978): *Innovation, the School and the Teacher.* Open University Press: Milton Keynes. A wide-ranging analysis of change in schools.
SHIPMAN, M. (1975): *Inside a Curriculum Project.* Longmans: London. An account with comments by those concerned of the development of one large curriculum project, namely the Schools Council's Integrated Humanities Project.

Other References

OWEN, J.H. and TISHER, R.P. (1978): 'Curriculum Adoption: The Fate of a National Curriculum Project in Australia', paper presented to AERA, 1978.
RAMSAY, G.A. (1972): 'Curriculum Development in Secondary School Science', *Quarterly Review of Australian Education* 5 (1) and (2).
TONKIN, C.B., ed. (1975): *Innovation in Social Education.* Pitmans: Carlton (Vic.).

7. *Whence and Whither the Australian Curriculum?*

A society in which education has become an important factor in social and moral life can no more abandon the educational system than it can the moral system itself to the absolutely arbitrary choice of individuals.

(E. Durkheim, 1977: 300)

In the last four chapters the framework and concepts developed in Chapter 2 have been used to organise historical material to try to answer the questions posed there concerning curricular change. These related to the manner in which the educational system was controlled, the allocation of resources, the changing social structure in which education was set, the ideologies current during the period, and to various curricular dimensions, particularly those relating to academic and moral teaching. In this final chapter some conclusions will be drawn from the analysis and, finally, an attempt will be made to say in which direction the Australian curriculum might move in the next two decades.

1. Development to Now

i)   The Changing Social Setting. As the salience of different social institutions has changed in Australian society so has the nature of the social relationships between those representing the interests of the various institutions. After the early military period the economy soon became the predominant institution and has remained prominent till now, although this salience has varied in character. One simple index of these changes is the varying proportion of those engaged in the primary, secondary and tertiary sectors in the labour force. The economy has switched from a rural emphasis to a manufacturing and, increasingly, to a service type economy, though because of the long Australian reliance on imports and exports there has always been a high proportion of the labour force in tertiary employment. Furthermore as the processes used in both industry and commerce have come to rely more and more upon science-based technologies of all types, the relevance, for the economy, of education has grown.

In the mid-nineteenth century the main ideology applied to the economy was that of *laissez-faire*. Certainly control of the economy by the Government was probably at that period at a minimum. Beforehand the military authorities controlled many prices and much of the overseas trade. Towards the end of the century, increasingly, control over wages, customs duties, and other economic matters led the economy away from strict *laissez-faire* in the direction of an economy managed, initially, in the interests of capital, though eventually constrained by the need to negotiate with the representatives of labour.

In this situation the capitalist class system, based within the growing Australian industrial framework, has become of growing importance. Clearly education has an important relationship with the social class system in that the schools can work to preserve class cultures and can also act as channels of entry to the high status positions in the economy around which advantaged class cultures are focused. An important part of the moral curriculum of an independent school is to ensure that social behaviour apt for the future member of the middle class has been learnt. In the state-provided schools the aim may be that, as far as possible, the identical curriculum and opportunities should be made available to all students, but the problem is that children arrive at school at the age of five with many vital attitudes and competences already well established so that they react differently to the experiences made available to them at school. The aim of the school can be perverted by social factors outside its control.

This is one of the main reasons why the family as a social institution is of great importance for education. Thus it is of great significance that the family has come to have a reduced salience in society as a whole during the last half century. Such functions as the preparation of the child as a parent or as a consumer have increasingly been handed to the school. Furthermore, as revealed religion has been given less credence over the last century, there have been no problems in the minds of many Australians in handing an increased responsibility for moral education to the schools. This is an ironic development since Australian state-provided schools are, in the main, secular. Hence they may not teach religion, but may teach, what for many is one of its main implications, morality.

Although these changes in the nature of the social structure have taken place, fundamentally Australian society has been very conservative—and this applies particularly to the polity. The political parties, whether called Labor or Liberal, have been conservative in orientation. Since federation the political system has taken to itself growing powers to control many aspects of society, including the economy. We live not under a system of *laissez-faire*, but in a society in which the aim is to achieve rational planning in the interests of the political party in power, while observing the constant necessity to negotiate with all possibly powerful interested parties. Such a system demands highly educated manpower to run the economy, but also demands a highly developed political commitment amongst its citizens.

Commitment to the political system was not originally a great problem in Australia, because the main source of inhabitants until about 1930 was the mother country of Britain. More recently a vast influx of migrants from such societies as Greece, Italy and Yugoslavia who have very different political systems has led to the end of the assumption that commitment to the Australian polity is automatic. In addition, there has been a radical change in the belief about the desirable nature of the Australian culture. First of all, there was an end to the conception of Australia as an Anglo-Saxon culture. Next, discussion was in terms of a multicultural society, but more recently the term coming to be used is 'polyethnic'. The aim has become, not assimilation into a slowly adapting Australian culture, but the coexistence in one society of many tolerated differences. Furthermore the Australian political conscience has become much more tender towards the plight of the Aborigines, and they, too, have come to be seen as a group to be accommodated within the diversity of Australian society.

The school curriculum is felt to have relevance to both the problems here highlighted in relation to the demographic structure. Thus political commitment has always been seen to be one quality that schools should ensure and the aim of a polyethnic society has clear implications for the content of curricula, especially in relation to language teaching and Social Studies lessons.

ii)   Changing Ideologies. The ways of justifying social and political actions in relation to education have changed greatly over the last two centuries. Firstly, in relation to the control of education the movement has been away from a more or less *laissez-faire* provision of schools to a situation where the State provides most of the schools, but, even where it does not do so, the independent schools are now operated under some controls by the State. Furthermore, since the 1870s when this policy was born, control has been centralised within each State, and in the last decade the Commonwealth Government has begun to exercise an increasing element of control, especially at the level of tertiary education.

The content of the curriculum has, however, been influenced by other changes in ideology. Three such changes have recently had a great effect. Firstly, there is the slow decline of the influence of the British connection; the feeling of Australian nationalism, itself always a complex factor, has grown stronger, particularly around the time of federation and also since World War II. The results for Australian culture are difficult to discern. The cultural basis from which selection has to be made in curricular planning has been influenced not merely by the new source of migrants, but also by the growing influence of United States' companies on the economy, particularly through the mass media. The other two important ideological changes relate as much to the moral as to the academic curriculum. There is the gradual decline in the willingness to grant deference to those in authority. A distrust of authority in moral and academic matters has become a mark of the last two decades. Australians have always, at least in myth, encouraged an antiauthoritarian spirit in relation to, for example, the boss or the police, but, nevertheless, the social structure has remained hierarchical, even if the social distance between the rungs and from top to bottom has been perceived as short. More recently, however, even minimal deference has been denied by those with more radical beliefs and, in addition, and particularly relevant to education, the authority of the universities in relation to creating and controlling the present paradigm of subjects has been questioned. This tendency leads to the third recent development. The concept of absolute truth in relation to both academic and moral knowledge has been increasingy questioned. Relativism rules and, since the individual is now often seen to be of more worth than any group, tolerance of individual differences in behaviour is to be encouraged.

Of the three ideological changes here described the growth of nationalism obviously owed much to local intellectuals. Thus the literary intellectuals connected with the *Bulletin* in the 1890s played a key role. But the other two changes, antiauthoritarianism and individualism, though latent in the Australian culture, were diverted in new directions by the ideas of such overseas intellectuals as Marcuse, even though the Australian involvement in the Vietnam war may have focused the changes in a particular way and at a particular time.

iii)   Changing Educational Ideas. There has, in other words, been a constant importing of ideas into Australia. Initially, the colonies were small, poor societies that, perforce, relied in many ways on Britain and could, or perhaps would, not support intellectuals. Those aspiring to an intellectual career, often at least initially, went overseas. Certainly in the field of education it was not until the interwar years that there were opportunities for educational intellectuals to play much part in Australia. Those who began at this time to think deeply and to apply their minds to the development of the curriculum in Australia inevitably travelled to Britain, the United States of America and, occasionally, to continental Europe, where they imbibed the new educational ideas of the times. They were, therefore, willing to promote a conference such as that run by the NEF in 1937, which relied for its strength on the bringing of educational intellectuals from overseas.

More recently communication has become so much improved that Australia's geographical isolation now means very much less. Ideas are transmitted so quickly around the world by the mass media and international travel is now so readily available that such educational ideologues as Ivan Illich can easily visit Australia to be questioned about how their ideas might apply here and also Australians can visit Illich in Mexico to clarify their view of his ideas before applying them in Australia. Therefore ideological shifts in educational ideas must now be seen in an international context; one can now say that Australia is part of the ideological context of so-called free societies. Thus a whole complex of educational ideas relating to antiauthoritarian and individualistic tendencies have become very strong in Australia, as they are throughout the Western world. These changes particularly relate to the importance given to the immediate experience of the individual child so that amongst those who support this ideology more attention must be given to the child creating his own view of knowledge rather than to all children being taught one view of social reality. For such persons this process of the child constructing his own view becomes the key concept around which curricula will emerge. No longer is the focus upon transmitting a previously determined set of knowledge to all children. An emergent, negotiated, individual curriculum is now seen by many as the necessary replacement for a curriculum based upon a common collection of agreed pieces of knowledge.

Such ideas are picked up by Australian educational intellectuals during their reading or visits overseas. These intellectuals have always, as in Britain, been members of bureaucracies and, therefore, have been liable to the formal and informal controls of the organisations of which they are members. Early in this century men like Tate and Board, administrators, acted to transmit new ideas, but were much constrained by the social roles that they had to play. By the interwar years Australian society had become wealthy enough to locate some intellectuals within the universities or in research bodies; G.S. Browne and K.S. Cunningham are examples. Since World War II the great growth of tertiary education, both in university faculties of education and in the former teachers colleges, has allowed the number of such intellectuals to rise. In addition, the greater administrative freedom recently granted to the teachers colleges withdrew many of the constraints formerly operating on their staff, previously members of Education Departments. Thus there is now a much bigger pool from which educational intellectuals may be drawn, though there has been no real tendency for such intellectuals to operate from non-official bases. Perhaps the only example of such 'free-floating' intellectuals may be found in such educational journalists as the late Henry Schonheimer in his writings for the *Australian* and Barry Hill, formerly of the *Age*.

However, one may ask how free most educational intellectuals really are. Universities can be seen as organisations licensed by society, in part, to be deviant, one of whose tasks it is to criticise society and suggest new ideas concerning the future directions and dimensions of change. But the ideas developed have to be taken up outside the tertiary sector and some modern educational ideas have been much opposed by society at large on the grounds, for example, that teachers should be making sure that the three R's are taught rather than allowing children to develop into creative illiterates.

Whatever will eventually be seen to be the best historical interpretation of the contemporary position of intellectuals, it can be said that there are few general intellectuals in Australia and that Australian educational intellectuals have always been and still are both very dependent upon imported ideas and largely employed within educational organisations of one sort or another—a fact that must constrain the nature of the suggestions for change that they make.

iv) *The Curriculum.* What may be called the Australian predicament has constantly changed over the last two centuries and has changed very often totally outside the control of those with power over the

Australian social structure. World economic depressions, political conflicts—especially leading to war—and ideological innovations overseas must affect Australia willy-nilly. Therefore the social factors operating upon the curriculum have been, and, as long as Australia remains a relatively open society, will continue to be, very largely outside the direct influence of those who control our educational system, although the ways in which these forces eventually affect the curriculum will be mediated by local conditions.

Because of the legacy from Britain, the way in which knowledge has been selected to form the school curriculum in Australia has tended to differentiate the elite from the masses. The needs of the largely mythical Australian emphasis upon egalitarianism were soon met by the establishment of mass elementary, later primary, education. As in many other societies, including the USSR and perhaps even China, the attempt to spread egalitarian opportunities in education into the secondary schools has run up against economic barriers of two sorts. The first related purely to the perceived costs of such an expansionary policy, but the second has proved equally important in Australia. Secondary, and indeed tertiary, education has come to be seen as vocational in aim. Therefore, in a country where rapid development has been considered vital, the curriculum has been influenced so that highest priority has been given to the largely vocational preparation of the élite rather than to the provision of mass general secondary education. Only very recently has this latter aim been seen as worthy of achievement and then largely by educational intellectuals rather than by those who control education or their masters, the electorate.

If the academic curriculum has been bent in this utilitarian direction so too has the moral curriculum been influenced in a somewhat similar manner. The legacy of payment by results in the elementary schools and the need for success in external examinations at various levels both in the independent schools, which originally supplied all secondary education, and in the more recently established state secondary schools have worked to change the moral lessons that the curriculum originally claimed to teach. These influences did not change the aim of producing dutiful citizens; if anything they ensured the success of this aim. But they did replace the hope that students would see service to others as a major moral quality with a competitiveness that was believed to be necessary if economic success, socially perceived to be crucial, was to be achieved. Yet here again the Australian spirit of egalitarianism has some influence. Success was to be achieved, but, where based on high quality, had to be disguised. Australian poppies may bloom in their thousands, but must not grow too tall.

2. Going Forward

i) The Stage of Meaning. In very recent years there has been a marked public reaction against the more permissive conceptions of education at present prevalent in many schools and there is a general feeling that whatever is done in schools a certain minimum level in the three R's should be achieved by all pupils. However the schools do seem to be putting a growing emphasis on the process, as opposed to the content, of learning—upon, for example, discovery and creativity rather than upon the details of what is to be learnt. Individual interpretation and understanding rather than conformity and memorisation seem to be the aim. Thus clearly many teachers are intent upon their students learning the meaning of the curriculum. Material may be essential to demonstrate the principles which are to be learnt, but there is no need for this mass of facts to be memorised. 'Meaning, not matter' seems to be the motto.

But one has to ask: meaning for what purpose? Beeby provided a means for analysing educational development whereby it was possible to show how teachers moved from a formally prescribed curriculum which might be learnt by rote to one that led to understanding. He did not, however, ask to what use the understanding should be put. In effect he ignored the moral component in the curriculum, but, as Durkheim noted in the quotation cited at the head of this chapter, those who control the schools, possibly under the prompting of those who pay for education, namely the voters, are hardly likely to put up with the teaching of a morality that binds students to destroy contemporary social norms.

The academic curriculum is still fundamentally in the control of the universities, because they guard the paradigms of existing subjects. Even if academic curricula were to emerge in progressive schools that were in opposition to contemporary versions of academic subjects the rational criticism of them by academics who opposed them would, in an open society, eventually bring these new curricula into derision, and force the teachers concerned back within the bounds of academic normality in the subjects concerned. However, the moral purposes to which such cognitive knowledge is put are not within the sole keeping of the universities and hence the meanings in service of which knowledge may be used can be influenced from within the schools or by the pressures of interest groups within the general public, who in their turn may influence the schools.

Agreement about such culturally defined purposes is rarely total, except perhaps at a time of crisis—a situation perhaps only experienced in Australia for a brief moment in the period 1942–44. Views about the solution of the contemporary national predicament are controversial. For example, the uses to which scientific knowledge concerning the environment should be put are many and various. Furthermore by the time a policy has been agreed upon the predicament itself may be altered by some such factor as the threat of a war, or a change in the world price of oil, or the invention overseas of some new relevant technology; in all these cases the determining factors would be outside Australian control.

It is because changes are inevitably with us that the social meaning of academic knowledge can never be final. Therefore the selection of the knowledge that is most relevant at any time or the best distribution of it must constantly be reconsidered and renegotiated by all those involved in education and in relevant social institutions. The best interpretation for us here of Beeby's concept of a stage of Meaning is that a curriculum is made available within which principles are emphasised, but in such a way that they are understood so firmly that they can be applied over a very wide range of likely situations. Thus technical apprentices should learn the principles of electric circuits and not how to wire up a bell as manufactured by a given company, or Domestic Science students should learn to cook, not to bake scones in an electric oven. But, in addition, meaning must be explored not merely in relation to cognition, but within the ever-changing relevancy of contemporary society and, therefore, within the moral norms currently operating in society. This does not mean that schools must not teach a new moral code or a new usage for some academic knowledge, but it does mean that when they do so they must expect to be challenged, to have to justify what they are trying to do and, finally, perhaps, to be stopped in their innovatory tracks by those with power over the educational system.

ii)   The Possible Future Social Setting. Given the present Australian social structure and the ideologies currently at work within this structure and given the pathway described in this book of how this point was reached, it may well be asked whether any predictions can be made of what social influences are likely to be at work on the curriculum over the next two decades or so. A brief attempt will be made here to make such a prediction and then to draw lessons from it for the future development of the curriculum in Australia.

The salience of the economy in the social structure has resulted in a society that, despite decreasing hours at work and the attendant increase in leisure, is so wealthy that Australia can now afford to pay what once would have been seen as a high wage to those who are unemployed. In Australia, as in most developed economies, there seems to be an increasing proportion of the labour force who are more or less permanently out of work due to structural changes in the economy. In other words one can envisage a movement towards a society in which a slowly increasing standard of life, together with greater leisure time, is sustained by a decreasing proportion of the total population. Such an economy can permit a proportion of the population to move out of the labour force either permanently or temporarily. The concept of a career or a life at work can be replaced by one of 'uncareer' (J. Hern, 1977), the basis of which would be the ability to contract out of the labour force, perhaps temporarily, and adopt an alternative mode of life with financial support from the State.

Yet to keep productivity high and maintain the level of sophistication of the economy there will still be a need for some career-oriented persons who will require a high level of education and training. Furthermore those who chose an uncareer will still need a basic education prior to making this choice for two reasons. Firstly, the choice is a difficult one demanding a real knowledge of alternatives and their possible results; secondly, the choice may be a temporary one and when persons opt back into the labour force an educational basis will be needed from which those concerned can take advantage of the available arrangements for continuing education to prepare themselves for entry or re-entry to the work force.

For one major reason this basic education must be general in nature. This is because economic change, which is often associated with technological or scientific change, is now rapid. Hence to educate for specific purposes prior to the minimum school leaving age is a recipe for creating trained incompetents when change occurs. However, to base all education, whether technical or professional, on general principles for as long as possible ensures that present students can adapt quickly to future conditions based on changes that are often unpredictable and usually outside Australian control. In the Australian situation there is one very major implication of this view, namely that there must be an end to the easy acceptance in schools of the long-established view that education should be utilitarian and vocational

This view can be seen not merely to be wrong, but to be positively harmful for matching education to the economy and to the needs of the next generation.

Though fewer may be employed in the economy, the proportion of the population still within the labour force will be great enough so that status in society will continue to be governed by inequalities at work. Since, under a semi-capitalist system, ownership of private property will very largely govern the nature of the economy, despite attempts to increase the participation of labour in the running of industry, a class-type system will remain. As a result the different cultures based on social class will retain their strength and their implications for differential success within the educational system. This is important at a time when the importance of the family will probably continue to diminish with the growing popularity of various alternative familial structures. In these circumstances the past tendency for the school to be expected to fulfil wide-ranging functions, because of the so-called failure of the family, is likely to remain strong.

Demographic and ideological forces will strengthen this remedial function of the school. Migrants of non-Anglo-Saxon background have begun to put demands upon the schools so that children from such families are given the same opportunities as those with Australian parents. Similar arguments have been advanced in relation to Aboriginal children. In both cases there are, in addition, political considerations. One may assume a continuance of our present version of democracy with perhaps more arrangements available for participation by citizens at the local level, but one cannot assume that migrant and Aboriginal elements will be automatically committed to this political system. The educational problem of helping to ensure political commitment to and participation in, a democracy, tolerant of ethnic differences, is one that at the level of curriculum Australians have only recently begun to face.

The changed demographic pattern and the increasing plea for tolerance of differences has one other structural implication and this relates to religion. Undoubtedly the salience of religion has lessened in Australia over the last century. Yet membership of the various Christian churches and the Jewish faith is still high. There are signs that greater tolerance is now being extended to religious differences and that this tendency is allowing those who are pressing for the teaching of religion in schools to overcome the long-established opposition to this form of instruction in Australian schools. The ideal of secular schools seems likely to be replaced by the chance for local option in the matter of religious education. If this is the case, the mechanics for making decisions about religion in schools will stand as a symbol of many of the structural and ideological changes in Australian society since its achievement will have been influenced both by demographic changes and by those ideological demands both of a political nature for greater participation by citizens and of a more general nature for the wider tolerance of individual differences.

iii) The Curriculum of the Future. In this social setting what curriculum may emerge? There is one cluster of ideological tendencies specific to education that must be considered, particularly in view of the fact that it is in opposition to another emerging political demand related to education. For a number of ideological reasons many teachers today emphasise that decisions about curriculum should be taken locally in schools, not centrally by state departments or by examination boards. In part this demand is seen as an index of professional freedom and in part it is connected with a radical political position concerned with individual freedom. This position, which has some strength in the secondary schools, especially perhaps in Victoria, is in direct opposition to the more conservative political demand for the greater accountability of the schools. There is an apparent confrontation here between educational intellectuals and many teachers, and politicians, especially of a conservative nature, and many voters.

A compromise may be possible if the curriculum is seen to consist of two parts, one of which is a basic core, whilst the other is negotiated within each school between teachers, students and parents, probably with the guidance of the principal. The core should be compulsory for all Australians and teachers would in some sense be accountable to representatives of society, possibly at the local level, to ensure that this was learnt by their students. The demands put upon the schools by the social structure would, in large part, control the content of this part of the curriculum. Teachers themselves would be responsible for the pacing of the material for groups or for individual students and for choosing the pedagogies to use for the various part of this core so that their method suited themselves and their students. On the other hand the negotiated part of the curriculum would emerge differently in each school and much of the need to meet the individual differences of students would be catered for in this part of the curriculum. Teachers would be professionally accountable for this content, though if they were to move outside the bounds tolerated by those in their own environments they might well be criticised and even checked in their plans. Indeed the realisation of such a possibility might well act to constrain the way in which they negotiated this second part of the curriculum.

The core must contain and give prominence to the three R's, which are basic to the rest of schooling and upon which much of the future life of all students must depend. The minimum necessary content of the syllabuses in the native tongue or in Arithmetic is a matter of empirical work which must take into account such findings as, for example, that most unskilled work can be done by those with a mental age of twelve. There are additional parts to this core. Clearly some elements of, for example, Science, Social Studies, and Physical Education must be included.

The case of Social Studies is an interesting one to examine in a little detail because recent research work carried out in Australia on what kind of learning about society is seen as essential (K.J. Piper, 1977) shows clearly the difficulties likely to be experienced in establishing the detailed content of any part of such a core curriculum. Piper found that the strongest general support came for teaching the skills involved in inquiry and decision making. There was less general support for teaching knowledge about concepts or information except where such cognitive material directly related to everyday living. The greatest disagreement concerned the teaching of values where differences were found between various groups involved in the study. Differences were found, for example, between, on the one hand, the academic camp of curriculum developers and teacher educators and, on the other, those who emphasised 'relevance', namely students, parents, teachers and employers.

In addition to the content already suggested, a case has been made that, since one of the main aims of the curriculum is to enable students to choose from all the knowledge that is available to the society, a certain minimum element of many of the possible types of knowledge must be taught in schools so that wise choices, based on adequate knowledge and experience, can be made (J.P. White, 1973). Thus, though it may be possible to decide whether or not to learn a foreign language as a result of the experience gained in learning one's native tongue, experience of one art form may be essential prior to making choices from all the contemporary art forms now available in our culture.

So far we have been considering only the academic curriculum, and the range of materials available to teach even the three R's is very great. Thus reading may be learnt by using bible stories, poetry, the

Women's Weekly, or the novels of D.H. Lawrence. In each case a different set of moral values is encompassed in the materials used so that the nature of the moral curriculum that will be taught in the core must be considered not only as a matter in its own right but in relation to the necessary delineating of the materials and also the pedagogies to be used for academic purposes.

In the tolerant ethos that characterises contemporary society, particularly as interpreted by many teachers, the moral values to be included in this core are hard to specify. Obviously tolerance itself is one such value, particularly as applied to ethnic groups and to political and religious beliefs. In addition, respect for human life and, in a participatory democracy, an acceptance that rational discussion rather than brute force should be used to settle differences are both core moral values. Yet the application in general living of the moral quality of tolerance, to which so much importance is now attached, raises the fundamental issue of how different people may be and remain members of Australian society. There must be some limit, or society itself will begin to break up because it lacks any binding norms; for example, attempts using violence to subvert democracy will almost certainly not be permitted. Thus, though tolerated differences will be allowed, even encouraged, loyalty to some conception of Australia must be expected and the schools will have their place in encouraging this fundamental political commitment.

The content of the negotiated part of the curriculum will depend upon a number of factors, but essentially upon the individual and the socially determined differences of students and of teachers. If a teacher is able and willing to teach some subject, then those students who wish to learn it and can wisely make a decision to do so should be able to do so. The personality, present competence and vocational wishes of students, the desires and beliefs of parents and of local citizens, the training to date and the professional ideologies of the teachers concerned will all play their part in the process of negotiating what emerges as the curriculum outside the core.

One last point must be emphasised: there can be no final decisions about the curriculum. This is perhaps truer of the negotiated part than of the core of the curriculum, but even in the latter part structural and ideological changes alter, not only the moral core and hence the materials used in the academic core, but also the demands put upon the schools concerning what scientific, for example, or other cognitive knowledge must be taught. Since such changes are inevitable, attention must be given to the ways in which necessary curricular change can take place. In the quotation at the head of this chapter Durkheim affirmed his belief in the need to manage the selection of knowledge made available through the schools to any society out of the total stock from which choice it may be made. We may conclude by a final quotation from Durkheim which shows his realisation that curricular change is always with us:

> For by showing that this moral order came into being at a particular time under particular circumstance, history justified us in believing that the day may eventually come when it will give way to a different moral order based on different ethical principles.
>
> (E. Durkheim, 1977: 329)

Although here Durkheim was specifically referring to change in the moral curriculum, his basic argument relates equally strongly to the academic curriculum. Because social change is inevitable all curricular decisions are provisional and this is the main reason why all teachers must have some expertise, if not in developing their own curricula, then at the very least in knowing how to chose between the alternative curricula that are offered to them.

Bibliography

WHITE, J.P. (1973): *Towards a Compulsory Curriculum.* Routledge & Kegan Paul: London. A perceptive, philosophical account of how decisions might be made as to the form of the core of the curriculum.

Other References

HEARN, J. (1977): 'Toward a Concept of Non-Career', *Sociological Review* 25 (2), 273–88.
PIPER, K.J. (1977): *Essential Learning About Society.* A.C.E.R.: Hawthorn (Vic.).

Index